HIDDEN TREASURES

WIGAN

Edited by Lucy Jeacock

First published in Great Britain in 2002 by
YOUNG WRITERS
Remus House,
Coltsfoot Drive,
Peterborough, PE2 9JX
Telephone (01733) 890066

HB ISBN 0 75433 838 X
SB ISBN 0 75433 839 8

FOREWORD

This year, the Young Writers' Hidden Treasures competition proudly presents a showcase of the best poetic talent from over 72,000 up-and-coming writers nationwide.

Young Writers was established in 1991 and we are still successful, even in today's technologically-led world, in promoting and encouraging the reading and writing of poetry.

The thought, effort, imagination and hard work put into each poem impressed us all, and once again, the task of selecting poems was a difficult one, but nevertheless, an enjoyable experience.

We hope you are as pleased as we are with the final selection and that you and your family continue to be entertained with *Hidden Treasures Wigan* for many years to come.

Contents

Garswood CP School

Andrew Pardoe	19
Michael Murray	19
Steven Elms	20
Jessica Vernazza	20
Kara Banks	20
Alex Neil	21
Sasha Amber Witherington	21
Jessica Wallace	21
Amy Thompson	22
Katie McAdam	22
Scott Robinson	23
Daniel Collins	23
Adam Chamberlain	24
Martin Reeves	24
Hannah McAdam	25
Nina Farley	25
Amanda Grace	26
Daniel Barton	26
Daniel Pennington	26
Charlotte Roby	27
Rachel Liptrot	27
Suzanna Randall	27
Adam Fairclough	28
Matthew Brown	28
Matthew Mitchell	28
Rachael Mitchinson	29
Hannah Farley	29
Zoe Smallshaw	29
Becky Frodsham	30
Kelly Miles	30
Nicholas Traynor	30
Sean Flaherty	31
Sam Bennett	31
Scott Davies	31
Mark Whelan	32
Aimee Dalton	33
Harriette Clark	34

Steven Cornish	69
Amelia Whittle	70
Naomi Myers	70

Parbold Douglas Primary School

Ben Holmes	70
Daniel Bates	71
Nicholas Rees	71
Adam Bennett	72
Tom Nelson	72
Emma Givens	73
James Ross	73
Kate Nelson	74
Nina Lee	74
Victoria Johnston	75
Michelle Fox	75
Sam Ward	76
Stephanie Woods	76

Rectory CE Primary School

Jonathon Speakman	77
Jordan Roberts	77
Emma Hilton	77
Lindsey Kay	78
Romy Stazicker	79
Amy Littler	80
Daniel Whitehead	80
Katie Lea	81
Hannah Lutas	81
Natasha Skupski	81
Leigh Taberner	82

R L Hughes Primary School

Alannah Maggs	82
Katie Smith	83
Matthew Birchall	84
Jack Wheeldin	85
Claire Dean	86

The Poems

Cool Friendship

Sharing moments,
Kind and caring,
Heartbreaking moments,
Truthful and honest,
Helping each other,
Silly seconds.
Days of enjoyment,
Smiley faces,
Good times,
Strong relationship,
Sharing games,
Everlasting kindness.
Manners and respect,
Kind and helpful,
Unforgettable memories,
Fun and games,
Playing together,
Trust always.
Crazy moments,
Treasured times to remember,
Brilliant times,
Shoulder to cry on,
Loving times to remember,
Strong feelings.
Fun and laughter,
Heartbreaking nights,
Mad times,
Manic moments,
Love will never end,
Forever friends.

Samantha Baldwin (10)
Abram CE Primary School

VIKINGS

Sea dogs,
Sea rovers,
Sea monster,
Sea dragon,
Longship,
Ship dodger,
Ship fighter,
Ship merchants,
Rapid raiders,
Sea slicer,
Longship,
Fortress maker,
Sea invaders,
Sea raiders,
Beast ships,
Beast of the sea,
Rowing ships,
Beast killer,
Sea lords.

Ben Peet (10)
Abram CE Primary School

FRIENDSHIP

Teamwork,
Good times,
Loving memories,
Silly seconds,
Sharing secrets.

Everlasting kindness,
Laughter,
Days of enjoyment,
A shoulder to cry on,
Forever friends.

Strong relationship,
Manners and respect,
Magical moments,
Kind and helpful,
Outburst of joy.

Loving and caring,
Respect opinions,
Playing together,
Joyful,
Support.

Amy James (11)
Abram CE Primary School

FRIENDSHIP

Sharing secrets,
Remembering some good times,
Having a shoulder to cry on,
A magical mate,
A helping hand,
Kind and loving,
With everlasting trust.

Sharing happiness,
Remembering those days of enjoyment,
Respectful,
And joyful,
Cheers you up when down,
Sharing toys, fun and games,
Strong relationship,
And wonderful ways.

Kirsty Rogerson (11)
Abram CE Primary School

Friends

Sharing fun,
Laughter lines,
Days enjoyment,
Smiley faces.

Silly seconds,
Good times,
Happy memories,
Teamwork.

Kind and helpful,
Loving and caring,
Unforgettable memories,
A shoulder to cry on.

Magical friendship,
Heartbreaking moments,
Everlasting kindness,
Helping hand.

Jade Slater (11)
Abram CE Primary School

A Red Dragon

I've found a dragon in my living room,
Very small and silent,
Red and white staring eyes,
Stomping around room to room,
Burning all the wires and cables,
All it eats is my teddies,
My best discovery yet!

Robert Bailey (10)
Abram CE Primary School

FRIENDS

Sharing fun,
Happy moments,
Sharing secrets,
Silly seconds,
Mad moments,
Sharing moments,
Loving trust,
Living times to remember,
Someone to talk to,
Strong relationship.
Brilliant times,
Days of enjoyment,
Everlasting trust,
Heartbreaking moments,
Heartbreaking nights.

Steven Wright (11)
Abram CE Primary School

DRAGON

Long, scaly body
Fire breathing breath
Huge, sharp claws
Long, spiky tail
Evil, glaring eyes
Needle-sharp teeth
Hissing red tongue
Ready to eat.

Katie Cottington (11)
Abram CE Primary School

Friends Forever

Special times,
Graceful moments,
Helping hand,
Loving and caring,
Helping and sharing,
Always there to help you.

A shoulder to cry on,
A hand to hold,
A mum to cuddle,
And a dad to kiss,
A life to love,
And a teddy to crunch.

Because a friend in need,
Is a friend indeed.

Dean Marsden (10)
Abram CE Primary School

Fierce Dragon

Four-legged creature,
Two, big green eyes,
One really long tail,
One fire-breathing nose.

Green, spiky body,
Pointy ears,
Sharp, white teeth,
Ten long claws.

Danielle Jones (10)
Abram CE Primary School

Cool Friendship

Loving times to remember,
Sharing good moments,
Unbreakable teamwork,
You'll have a shoulder to cry on,
You can be happy and sad with your friends,
Good times to spend with them,
Tragic moments to share,
Heartbreaking times to tell about,
Treasuring times to remember,
Everlasting times,
Sharing moments,
Helping with homework,
Sharing your games and toys,
Sharing secrets,
Crazy moments,
Love will never end.

Amy Wilde (11)
Abram CE Primary School

The Vikings

Muscles like rock,
mighty warriors,
they wear strong armour,
they have snappy swords,
shout like roaring wolves,
they have very loud horns,
they always wear sandals,
and have metal hats,
it's war day every day!

Nadine Williams (10)
Abram CE Primary School

My Best Friend

Kind and caring,
Loving and sharing,
Trusting and grateful,
Laughter and fun,
Magical friendship.
Great times,
Interesting memories,
Heartbreaking moments,
Smiling faces,
Sharing good moments.
Enjoying games,
Silly seconds,
Days of enjoyment,
Love will never end,
Always best friends.

Leonie Smallwood (10)
Abram CE Primary School

Vikings

Warrior raiders,
Rabid demons,
Smooth criminals
Masters in disguise,
Crafty vultures,
Against settling,
Blood bathers,
Slaughtering kings,
The crowned traders,
Violence seekers.

Nicholas Owen (10)
Abram CE Primary School

Everlasting Friends

Happy memories,
Graceful moments,
The good times,
Having fun,
Being helpful.

Heartbreaking seconds,
Strong relationships,
Loving each other,
Helping others,
Help in hand,
Sharing feelings.

Ryan Jones (11)
Abram CE Primary School

Good Friend

Kind and caring,
Fun and helpful,
Sharing all your secrets.

Brilliant memories,
Happy times,
Magical moments.

A day's enjoyment,
Fun and laughter,
Happiness all the time.

Daniel Jones (11)
Abram CE Primary School

SHIPS

Dragons of the sea,
Longboat leaders,
Sea roamers,
Strong mast,
The sea wagon,
The sea masters,
Dodging longboats,
Lions of the sea,
Demons of the deep,
Long serpent ships.

Darryl Forshaw (10)
Abram CE Primary School

VIKINGS

Mighty warriors,
Sea robbers,
Leaders of the sea,
Sea rovers,
Killers of the sea,
Superb seamen,
Country killers,
Traders of these,
Jewel demons,
Ship builders.

Adam Bridge (11)
Abram CE Primary School

FRIENDSHIP

Brilliant moments,
Strong relationship,
Mad minutes,
Silly seconds,
A shoulder to cry on,
Loving and caring,
Sharing celebrations,
Days of enjoyment,
Sharing fun,
Heartbreaking nights.

Claire Belshaw (11)
Abram CE Primary School

VIKINGS

Sea robbers,
Island invaders,
Smooth criminals,
Fierce fighters,
Sea traders,
Boat makers,
Rapid fighters,
Slippery beasts,
Mad invaders,
Sea explorers.

Ryan McKenzie (10)
Abram CE Primary School

They Stand And They Plot

Three German troopers stand and plot
Thinking of how they can get past the English
Most men are dead, there is hardly a lot
Scheming about how they can put down mines
You have to be careful with a German mind
But still they stand and they plot

Three German troopers stand and they plot
Thinking about their families that they left
Even more men are dying second by second
Every day millions of men are wounded
Even though the English are bombing
They still stand and still plot

Three German troopers stand and they plot
Still standing and plotting about something
English dropping mustard bombs all around
The Germans are wearing their gas masks
Until one day England decide to end the war
Nobody is standing, nobody is plotting.

John Webster (10)
Billinge St Aidan's CE Primary School

War

People sitting, watching and waiting,
waiting for others to come.
When they come, the fight will be brutal
sadly, many will die.

People looking, kneeling with guns
sounds of gunfire, sounds of bombs.
Unfortunately, the fight will make lives lost
sadly, a lot will die.

People shooting at others they hate
dying bodies, serious wounds.
The horror of it shocked everyone
sadly, many have died.

Michael Hawkins (10)
Billinge St Aidan's CE Primary School

HUSTLE AND BUSTLE

Hustle and bustle in the city
All a big rush to get out of town
All the children carrying their bags
Onto the bus to get away
Hustle and bustle in the city

Hustle and bustle in the city
The bus starts to move away
Out of the city
And into the country
Excitement builds in the bus

Hustle and bustle in the city
Speeding up into the country
Finally safe
Out in the country
Peace and quiet in the country

Peace and quiet in the country
The children rush off the bus
Happy and safe
Peace at last
Peace and quiet in the country.

Matthew Haslam (10)
Billinge St Aidan's CE Primary School

Knitting A Boy

She sits and she knits,
All alone, she starts,
First its head
And she sits and she knits.

She sits carefully watching,
Watching her so small careful hands,
Listening to the needles clicking together
And she sits and she listens.

She sits and she knits,
Nearly finished now,
Happy and pleased with herself for her work
And she sits and she knits.

Now she's finished her work of knitting
Her so unreal boy.

Victoria Barker (11)
Billinge St Aidan's CE Primary School

A Frosty Morning

The trees are golden brown
And the cool breeze blows through my hair,
The leaves make a swishing sound,
Then all is calm, all is still.

The river beside me is frozen
And I'm slip sliding on the icy path,
The birds sing a song as I walk past,
Then all is calm, all is still.

The field beside me is frosty
And the cows are nowhere around,
The spiders' webs are glistening in the sunshine,
Then all is calm, all is still.

Louise Wright (11)
Billinge St Aidan's CE Primary School

WELCOME HOME TIM

Tim was coming home this afternoon
He had been at war
His wife and baby waited for him
Along with crowds of people
Cheering as he came
Tim was home.

Outside his house was a banner saying
Welcome home Tim
With streamers and flags waving everywhere
Getting in everyone's way
But no one cared
Tim was home.

Everyone was waving, happy as anything
His wife was smiling
Holding his baby boy
The crowd all wanted to cheer him on
He was a saviour
Tim was home.

Emily Hetherington (11)
Billinge St Aidan's CE Primary School

FOOTBALL

Football is good
Play any time
It's only a bit of mud
So make the ball mine
So if the weather is good or bad
Play anyway
And don't get mad
Go training, pay one pound a week
Don't cost you much
So get out there and kick with your feet
Golden feet
Make it count
After all you are the best.

Dean Brady (10)
Billinge St Aidan's CE Primary School

DARKNESS

Darkness,
From sundown,
It engulfs the world.
Darkness,
Deadly and intoxicating.
It dwells in corners,
Concealing what
Is hidden within.
Darkness,
Lying to your eyes
And deluding the mind.
Darkness,
Until the morning dawns.

David Hitchcox (11)
Billinge St Aidan's CE Primary School

He Stands And He Waits

He stands and he waits,
For the outstanding pose.
Sighting his camera,
He stands and he waits.

He leans and he takes,
Asking for another.
Taking his last,
He leans and he takes.

He stands and he packs,
Getting out his box.
Taking down his camera,
He stands and he packs.

Antony Chadwick (11)
Billinge St Aidan's CE Primary School

War

Sandbags everywhere,
Mortar shells stacked up high.
War planes and army bombers
Soaring through the sky.
'Rifles at the ready!'
The general would shout.
If I could be the general,
I'd give him a clout.
Planes soaring everywhere,
Filling up the sky.
Bombs almost jumping
Out of bombers flying high.

Daniel Comish (10)
Billinge St Aidan's CE Primary School

END OF THE WAR

Two men walking down Portman Street,
After bombs and guns killed families.

Screams and bombs couldn't be heard anymore,
The street was quiet; the war had finished,
Two soldiers were walking down the street,
Cheers of joy, waiting to get home.

Children waiting for their dads to come home,
Mothers waiting for their husbands.
Welcome home!
The village cheered to them.

They were home, smiles
Appeared on people's faces.
They didn't care why or what
He had come home for, they just cheered
And kids' faces were soon happier.

Amalia Teix (11)
Billinge St Aidan's CE Primary School

KNITTING

She sits and she knits
In a world of her own.
Starting from the head,
Quickly working her way down
And she sits and she knits.

She sits and she thinks
About what to do next.
She's lost her book,
Looking everywhere with still no sign
And she sits and she thinks.

She jumps with joy,
She's found her book and finished knitting.
She tries it on and rips it,
She's very upset
And she cries with laughter.

Andrea Marshall (11)
Billinge St Aidan's CE Primary School

Dinosaur!

Giant meat eater,
Attacks its prey,
Enormous,
Scary,
Dangerous,
Unkind,
Feels ready to eat
Extinct.

Andrew Pardoe (10)
Garswood CP School

My Bed

Big and puffy,
Long and fluffy,
My Ted and me
Snuggle up in it at night,
Worried about the height,
Never alone,
In my peaceful night-time home.

Michael Murray (11)
Garswood CP School

Chocolate

C hocolate chewy, tasty.
H ave a bit
O f this lovely caramel delight.
C ome and enjoy the Cadbury's World.
O range chocolate melts in your mouth.
L ovely chocolate from the south.
A ll the chocolate is so delicious.
T o my surprise I like it all.
E at and enjoy more.

Steven Elms (9)
Garswood CP School

Puppy

P uppies are cute and cuddly
U nbelievably playful
P lenty of energy to play
P eering through the door at night
Y ou really think they're *great!*

Jessica Vernazza (9)
Garswood CP School

Farms!

F ields of ripe green grass
A pples of kinds hanging from enchanting trees
R olls of golden hay everywhere
M arvellous animals in curious barns
S melly scents here and there.

Kara Banks (10)
Garswood CP School

THE UNIVERSE

U niverse is large, further than the eye can see
N ebulas big, creating stars.
I nside a galaxy planets, stars and asteroids
V ery large, ever expanding
E nding nowhere in sight
R ed giant stars, ready to explode
S upernova, blasting giant rocks
E verlasting, living for all time.

Alex Neil (10)
Garswood CP School

FLOWER

F antastic smell
L ovely colours
O ver the top, hovering are bees
W ater is sprinkled on them every day
E very day bees come to visit
R oses, they are!

Sasha Amber Witherington (9)
Garswood CP School

SPORT

S is for swimming in the swimming pool
P is for polo that makes it really cool
O is for Olympics get running and trying hard,
R is for rugby play it in the backyard,
T is for tennis that sport is the best,
north, south, east and west.

Jessica Wallace (9)
Garswood CP School

Day!

Monday,
Back a day.
Sunday,
Skip a day.
Tuesday,
Next day.
Wednesday,
Jump a day.
Friday,
Back a day.
Thursday,
Skip a day.
Saturday,

One week covered.

Amy Thompson (11)
Garswood CP School

Rabbit

Fast runner
Big leaper.

Leave eater
Cat hater.

Cute sleeper
Nut keeper.

Leg stretcher
Dog hater.

Katie McAdam (11)
Garswood CP School

Turtle

Hard shell
Soft bell
Slow walker
Quiet talker
Quick swimmer
Water shimmer
No strengths
Swim lengths
No slipper
Double clipper
Hides away
Never stay
Under barge
Camouflage
Weak body
Never noddy!

Scott Robinson (10)
Garswood CP School

Monkey

Swinging on trees
chewing on leaves
playing games on the frames
tree swingers
banana bringers
kind and mischievous
don't you think?
Really noisy
squeeze the trees
dinner time
fruit and leaves.

Daniel Collins (11)
Garswood CP School

A DRAGON'S TALE

Scales like polished bronze,
Breathe as hot as a volcano's fire,
Eyes the size of a warrior's shield,
Teeth like stalagmites in a dark cave,
A blood-red tongue as hot as lava,
Leathery bat like wings,
So large they could black out the sun,
Flies like a silver arrow,
Walks slyly like a hunting fox,
Guarding his treasure jealously,
Leaving it only for food and more gold,
How long is a dragon's tale?
It's as long as the tail of the dragon.

Adam Chamberlain (10)
Garswood CP School

TRAINS

O ven glowing
N ails working

T rains on track
R oads by cars
A cid train
N ight-time
S hops in dark
P eople walking
O il and diesel
R ail freight trains
T rams' trail.

Martin Reeves (10)
Garswood CP School

Witches Potion

Eye of a newt and tongue of a dog
Toe of a human and part of a log.

Walking round the cauldron thrice
One of the witches stirs it nice.

Bubble, bubble oil and gunge,
Tails of a mice, pigs and lice
Go in with a plunge.

A blind worm's sting
And a howlet's wing.

Add thereto a tiger's chauldron
For the ingredient of our cauldron.

Bubble, bubble oil and gunge,
Tails of a mice, pigs and lice
Go in with a plunge.

Hannah McAdam (11)
Garswood CP School

School Days

Hurry up, last minute rush.
Get into class, sit down and hush.
Get out your books, pencils and pens,
And give in our homework report on hens.
Sit on the carpet and do some maths,
Then after dinner we go to the swimming baths.
We go home out the gate,
Then into bed by half-past eight.

Nina Farley (11)
Garswood CP School

LION!

Lion,
Fierce roar,
Meat-eating creature
Ferocious, angry, wild, uncivilised,
Sly!

Amanda Grace (9)
Garswood CP School

OWL

Owl,
old owl,
faces all around,
loves the gloomy sky,
wise.

Daniel Barton (9)
Garswood CP School

FIREWORK

Fantastic exciting,
Swirls, twirls, curls,
Wonderful, amazing, colourful, dazzling,
Bang!

Daniel Pennington (9)
Garswood CP School

SNAKE

Long, legless,
slivers, squirms
soft, scaly,
dry eyes
snake.

Charlotte Roby (10)
Garswood CP School

LABRADOR

Soft, cuddly,
desperate for walks.
Warm, fluffy to touch,
friendly.

Rachel Liptrot (10)
Garswood CP School

LION

Fiercely stalking
Catching its prey
Pouncing through the Serengeti
Growl!

Suzanna Randall (9)
Garswood CP School

HAMSTER

H airy and furry as can be,
A lways needs lots of company,
M y best friend,
S illy as my brother,
T iny as a ring,
E veryone likes to sing to her,
R oly-poly.

Adam Fairclough (9)
Garswood CP School

PLANETS

P luto, Saturn, Jupiter and more
L onely in the midnight sky
A ll standing still and firm
N eptune, Earth, Uranus and more.
E xcitement on only one planet.
T errestrials studying the Earth below.
S omewhere something lurks.

Matthew Brown (10)
Garswood CP School

WINTER

W hat a chilly time of year
I s the winter when the trees are bare?
N othing grows at that time
T he stockings are up for Christmas Eve
E veryone's excited
R eindeer get ready for that magical day.

Matthew Mitchell (8)
Garswood CP School

Christmas

C rackers exploding around the dinner table.
H olly decorating your home with its green, spiky leaves.
R eindeer prancing on the roof pulling Santa's sleigh.
I cing on the Christmas cake, yum!
S tockings hanging by the fire hoping to be filled.
T he toys received make smiling faces.
M istletoe is where the boys and girls kiss.
A ngels hovering high above.
S anta who makes Christmas an exciting time!

Rachael Mitchinson (10)
Garswood CP School

Faces

F aces are all different
A ppearing everywhere
C lean and dirty
E yes on a face can scare or glare
S ad or smiling.

Hannah Farley (9)
Garswood CP School

Ladybird

Red-spotted,
Hovering, fluttering, tiny,
Delicately flying, here, there,
Ladybird.

Zoe Smallshaw (10)
Garswood CP School

Christmas

C rackers are put on the tree at Christmas
H olly hanging from the door
R obin twittering in the sky
I cicles hanging from the gutters
S nowflakes falling from the sky
T oys being delivered from Santa
M istletoe hanging from the ceiling
A ll the presents round the tree
S anta flying through the sky.

Becky Frodsham (9)
Garswood CP School

Seasons

In autumn the leaves fall from the trees.
In winter the ponds begin to freeze.
In spring the frogs lay their spawn,
And baby lambs are born.
In summer the sun begins to shine,
And everyone feels fine.

Kelly Miles (8)
Garswood CP School

Candle

Flickering little candle
Burning through the night
Lit by a single flame
Hanging on with all its might.

Nicholas Traynor (10)
Garswood CP School

STARS

Bright star out at night
Shedding off a burning light
What a pleasant sight.

Up in the dark sky
Twinkling like a little eye
Watching life go by.

Sean Flaherty (10)
Garswood CP School

LIMERICK

There was a man from Bengal
Who fell off a wall
He broke his leg
And laid an egg
But didn't care at all.

Sam Bennett (10)
Garswood CP School

SNAKE

Python,
Slimy, snake
Squeezing, slowly sideways
Scared, senseless, speechless, helpless
Sssssshhhhhh!

Scott Davies (9)
Garswood CP School

AUTUMN TREES

Autumn is here,
The leaves are changing colour
To look like a rainbow.
The colours of the leaves
Are very, very different.
Red, brown, gold and russet.
Tinges of green are hard to find.
The trees look on fire
With all the autumn colours.
The colourful leaves
Float gracefully to the floor
Twirling and swirling
Rocking and twisting,
Swaying and gliding,
Slowly to the ground,
Like paper helicopters.
Landing gently on the floor
Making a huge, colourful carpet.
Toadstools popping up
At the roots of the tree.
Birds are standing
On the branches
Empty and bare
The trees
Look like bony fingers
Waiting for winter
Autumn
is here
Winter
is approaching
fast.

Mark Whelan (9)
Garswood CP School

AUTUMN IS APPROACHING

Autumn is approaching!
The trees are very colourful
with reds, yellows, golds and browns
like bonfires flashing brightly.
The trees are getting more beautiful
and more beautiful.
The trees are getting bare
as the leaves start falling gently
to the wet ground.
As they fall
they twist and turn,
hovering over the brightly
looking trees.
They glide
and sway
until they touch
the hard, muddy earth.
The ground
is covered
with a colourful carpet.
Children come kicking
the crunchy leaves.
The leaves curl
up like cuddling rabbits.
A lovely, colourful
rainbow is scattered
on the green grass.
As the season changes
winter is here.

Aimee Dalton (9)
Garswood CP School

AUTUMN'S COLOURS

Autumn is here,
With leaves changing,
Red, gold and brown,
Like a burning fire
In the air.
Then they all fall
Twirling in the air,
Swirling like
Ballerinas.
Gliding, hovering,
Spinning and twisting
On the damp ground.
Sometimes,
You may see,
A tinge of green,
On the ground,
Like a
Big rainbow carpet.
Sometimes soggy,
Sometimes crunchy,
Children stand
On the colourful leaves,
Crunching and crackling.
Trees are now
Becoming bare.
Winter
Is drawing near.
Autumn's
A colourful
Time of year.

Harriette Clark (9)
Garswood CP School

HARVEST IS BACK

Harvest time
Is back again.
Massive yellow combine harvesters
Like starving dragons
With metal jaws
Cutting down
The golden corn,
With spinning blades
Frightening animals
Throwing out
Bundles of hay.
Bright red apples
Falling from the trees.
Scrappy scarecrows
Stood up straight
Trying to frighten
The birds away.
Farmers in their tractors
Digging up juicy vegetables.
Ready for cold winter.
Tasty wheat and corn
Blowing slowly
In the wind.
Farmers finishing
Off their work.
Children making
Corn dollies
With bits of hay
They have found.

Rachel Scott (9)
Garswood CP School

HELLO HARVEST

Harvest time!
Harvest time!
Apples are so juicy
and start falling to the ground,
and terrified animals
scatter around the fields
to get away from the
red shining tractor,
the tractor with the very
sharp teeth indeed.
The farmer's work is very, very hard.
He comes back in
exhausted with a very sore back,
with his hard day's work
on the fields.
There are vegetables
which the farmer gets out
off the ground.
There are wheat, oats,
potatoes, carrots, hay
and corn.
Tattered scarecrows
stuck into the ground.
Children in the haystacks
throwing the hay.
Farmers get ready
for the next day.
Harvest time is here!

Laura Clisham (9)
Garswood CP School

AUTUMN TREES

Autumn's here!
Leaves are changing colour.
Red, yellow
and a hint of green
like traffic lights.
Russet, orange and brown,
burning bright
like a bonfire.
The leaves swirl
gracefully to the
damp ground.
Hovering and spiralling
like a helicopter,
spinning like a ballerina.
A colourful carpet of leaves
on the ground,
children kicking
and crunching all around.
Trees are bare
like skeleton fingers.
The brittle branches
like witches' bones.
As the season dies
the leaves rot away
like old wood and flesh.
Winter is close, very close!

Adam Davies (10)
Garswood CP School

The Four Seasons

Spring is bouncy
It's lovely to watch
Animals are born
And eggs all hatch.
Plants all grow
There's no more snow!

Summer is hot
In a flower pot
It's hot when you're even outside
Let's go to the pool
Summer's so cool.

Autumn is fun
Leaves can weigh a ton.
Let's go and bounce
And pounce
In the leaves.

Winter is cold
It can be fun.
If you don't catch a cold
When you're out.
Watch out
It can be slippery on the road
For the old.

Abigail Mills (8)
Garswood CP School

THE HARD-WORKING MONTHS

The hard-working months are here
again, combine harvesters are
in the fields, like big, fiery
monsters with big, jagged teeth
gobbling up corn.
Terrifying small
helpless animals.
Big, juicy apples
fall off their branches
suddenly.
Hay and barley sway in
the breeze slowly and softly.
Big bundles of wheat in round
circle heaps.
Children laugh
and cheer
having a great
jolly time.
Field mice
and other
animals make
their new homes.
The hard-working
months are here again.

Christopher Simpkin (10)
Garswood CP School

My Dog Patch

Patch the puppy
is fun and bouncy
such a cute, little puppy
all soft and fluffy.

Black and white
such a wonderful sight
I would never give him up
for a king or queen's cup.

Patch is so small,
but it doesn't really matter.
He loves to go to the mall
as long as I'm there
For all that matters
I love my dog
Patch!

Lauren Spanner (7)
Garswood CP School

Hair Gel

Hair gel is a great invention,
If your hair needs some attention,
Slap it on and you will see
How good-looking cool can be!

Put it on your lovely curls,
Go out to impress the girls.
Hair gel is the best for you,
Don't get it mixed up with
Sticky glue!

Hannah Robinson (10)
Garswood CP School

The Deep Blue Sea

The deep blue sea,
It's calm and quiet.
The ocean's waves roar upon the sand,
The sea has lots of shells.
People surfing the rough waves,
Blue as the sky.

The sea is like a paradise,
Mussels and cockles,
People digging sandcastles.

The deep blue sea.

Rebecca Buckley (11)
Hindley Green CP School

The River

The river,
The long river flows.
Peaceful, quiet and long,
And people go to sing a song.
It is like a snake
And it's like water coming
Out of the tap.
I feel very peaceful when I see it.
I feel like I am the river.
The river,
It makes me think of a drink.

Ross Thomasson (10)
Hindley Green CP School

THE TRAVELLER

It was a dark, stormy night,
As I galloped along the road.
The moon was blinking and the shadows were listening.
The wind whistled through the clouds,
It blew the leaves into my face,
I rode faster and faster,
The wind blew harder as though it was trying to catch me.
I could see the house in the distance,
I slowed down and the leaves scuttled past.
I got off my horse and walked up to the old gates,
It was silent all around,
I called,
'I'm back, I kept my promise,'
The wind blew
And nobody retrieved my call.

Jessica Crosby (11)
Hindley Green CP School

THE LIGHTNING

The lightning
Lights up the trees
Bright, deadly, fierce
Like the sea roaring,
Like a light flickering
It makes me feel scared
Like a tree burning down.
The lightning
Shows us nature's strength.

Hayley Chapman (10)
Hindley Green CP School

THE GRAVEYARD

Searching the graveyard,
in the dead of night.
Creeping silently,
we could hear everything.
Suddenly we heard a rustle in the trees,
we turned quietly.
We heard it again . . .
footsteps and rustling like crumpled
up newspaper.
It seemed that the graves were moving slowly.
Something touched me,
a cold shiver ran down my back.
I turned around,
there was standing a horrible, messy man,
with an axe.
I ran for my life.

Daniel Worthington (10)
Hindley Green CP School

A COOL ICE CREAM

An ice cream
A very cool and refreshing snack
Cool, icy, creamy
It runs down the cone like gravy on chips.
It melts in your mouth like a cube of ice.
It makes me feel refreshed
As though I have just dived into a pool.
An ice cream
It makes me think about summer.

Lauren Bostock (10)
Hindley Green CP School

The Sea

The sea
The salt water that covers most of
The Earth's surface.
Huge, deep, murderer
Like a giant puddle.
Like a huge glass of blue pop.
It makes me feel great
Like a goldfish in a tank.
The sea,
Keeps us alive.

Phillip Sutton (10)
Hindley Green CP School

The Snake

The snake
A fierce jungle creature
Wild, violent, great
Moving fast like a train
Sliding like engine oil
I like its skin
It's soft and dry
The snake
Choking the tree trunks.

Daniel Turner (11)
Hindley Green CP School

The Sky

The sky
The sky looks blue
It's got the colour of the sea
It always has lots of different cloud shapes.

It is like the sea
The clouds are like cotton wool
When I look at it it makes me feel peaceful
The sky
The sky makes me think of the sea.

Jennifer Grogan (10)
Hindley Green CP School

THE PIG

The pig
It plays all day
Feeding, pushing, running
Like a puppy playing
Like a cat running
It makes me feel happy
The pig
A noisy farmyard pet.

Jamie Davies (11)
Hindley Green CP School

THE LION KING

The lion,
King of the jungle
Powerful, mighty, violent
Like an emperor in charge of land,
Like a boxer fighting,
It makes me feel small,
Like a speck of dust.
The lion king,
Shows how the jungle is ruled.

Anneka Wannakukorale (10)
Hindley Green CP School

I Did

The last gun sounded, the last man died,
Now home, home to my love,
Back to my home town,
The night was black,
Moon a yellow glow,
Hoof against stone,
Stone against hoof,
The ghostly outline of my home,
Paint worn off the bracken door,
'Whoa, boy!' the horse stopped,
I knocked for the one I love,
No answer,
No answer,
The trees whispered.
I rang the bell for the one I love,
No answer,
No answer,
The trees whispered,
'But I promised to come back!'
I did ,
I did.

Emily Beachcroft (10)
Hindley Green CP School

Motorbike Poem

Motorbike,
You ride on it.
It's got two wheels.
It's got two mudguards.
It also has stickers.
It's like a bike.

It's like a car too because it has an engine.
It races me from one place to the other.
It makes me feel excited too.
Motorbike,
It makes me think of trees passing by.

Christopher Smith (10)
Hindley Green CP School

The Great White Shark

The great white shark
The king of the sea.
Ferocious, strong, great,
Like a missile from a submarine.
Like a fast sports car
It makes me feel weak,
Like a growing plant.
The great white shark
It makes me think of nature and
What has been killed by it.

Scott Edgington (11)
Hindley Green CP School

Aeroplane

The aeroplane
It flies,
It carries passengers,
It goes fast and travels through the air.
It's like a bird and like a rocket,
They make me feel happy,
The aeroplane,
Reminds me of wings.

Daniel Peter Gilbert Betts (11)
Hindley Green CP School

The Wind

The wind never stops blowing strong or slow.
Mighty, strong, aggressive,
Like a force pushing and pushing.
Like hundreds of warrior soldiers
Running at speed for battle.
It makes me feel scared and weak.
It makes my legs feel like jelly
The wind
Shows you that it is there.

Scott Arkwright (11)
Hindley Green CP School

The King Of The Jungle

The lion
The king of the jungle
Strong, fierce, ferocious.
He runs like the wind
And hunts like a snake.
I think the lion is great
It makes me feel like a worm.
A lion
It makes me think about other animals.

Bradley Hargreaves (10)
Hindley Green CP School

The Thunder Cloud

The thunder cloud
A clump of static electricity
Big, black, wild
Like a candle in the sky,
Like a giant storming by.

It makes me feel small
Like a bug to a plant
The thunder cloud
Clearing the air.

Matthew Paul (10)
Hindley Green CP School

The River

The river is blue and full of fish,
It is just like a big blue dish.
It is long but narrow,
But fatter than a sparrow.
It is the longest in the world,
And it is very curled.
It is good for fishing,
And the water is always swishing.
It smells like the sea,
And it is great fun for me.

Alex Strickland (10)
Hindley Green CP School

The Dog

The dog,
Standing next to its owner
Strong, proud, protective,
Like a brave lion,
Like a soldier on guard.
It makes me feel safe
Like a baby in its mother's arms.
The dog,
Man's best friend.

Lee Davies (11)
Hindley Green CP School

THE COUNTRY AND CITY

Travelling fast on a top class train,
People outside all covered in rain,
Splash, splash going through puddles,
Drivers in traffic all in a muddle.

Children and parents all under a tunnel,
Pitch-black as dark as the train's funnel,
A clown entertained the children's dull faces,
As little, old people walked slow paces.

Past a tall skyscraper nearly touching the sky,
People were shouting loudly 'Oh my!'
Now going faster at 40mph,
Zooming past a really tall tower.

Now slowing down again out of the city,
People on the train said 'Oh what a pity,'
Into the countryside we now go,
The train chugging along, now getting slow.

Home now, home we go,
On the train nice and slow,
Back at the station we get off the train,
Ready to walk home in the rain.

Open the door walk into the house,
Not a sound as quiet as a mouse,
Settle down into the chair,
Get out a towel and dry your hair.

Lying on the couch breathing fast,
'Yes, yes home at last!'

Danielle Foster (10)
Hindley Green CP School

A Tyrannosaurus Rex

A Tyrannosaurus Rex,
The king of the dinosaurs
Monstrous, gigantic, destructive,
Like a killing giant beast,
Like a mountain,
It makes me feel strong,
Like a lion scraping for meat
A Tyrannosaurus Rex,
King of the world.

Peter Davies (11)
Hindley Green CP School

The Football Match

The fans crowd in coughing and groaning,
They make their way up the silent stairs,
And all you hear is the 'click, clock, click, clock'
of their footsteps.
Talking and walking, whispering and nattering.
Clicking and clocking, muttering and splattering.
The teams are out, the match has begun.
Whistling and cheering, chanting and groaning.
Spitting and spluttering, snorting and moaning,
Shooting and scoring, sprinting and tricking,
Passing and crossing, throwing and missing,
Swearing and booing, commenting and songs,
Roaring and screaming, crying and screeching.
The full-time whistle has gone, the home team
have lost, they're booing and swearing,
And moaning and groaning, crying and sobbing,
And walking and talking.
Will they be back next time?

Scott Cummins (10)
Holy Family RC Primary School

Theme Park

Morning approaches,
Rides clanking,
Followed by the sound of the cars pulling up.
The boss shouting, ill-tempered,
Hot under the collar . . .

Owners of the rides,
Ordering, shouting, full of danger.
Boss riding and pushing,
Up come the rides.

The rides open with loads of eager,
Excited faces gawping.
Rushing, running, pushing starts again
As the crowd turns in.
Stand back! Stand back!

The clanking starts again as the rides are moved away,
Chattering and nattering, clanking and stomping,
Stamp! Stamp!

The feet of the angry tired owners gathering,
Shouting, anger raging.
Soon it goes quiet,
Too quiet, until the next day begins.

Laura Gallagher (9)
Holy Family RC Primary School

Haiku

Waterfall gliding
Waterfall falling below
Waterfall sliding.

Hannah Capner (9)
Holy Family RC Primary School

Shopping Centre

Children crying, children moaning, 'Can I have that?
Please. It's getting cold put your coat on.
Come on let's go and get warm.'
Talking, chattering, young ones nattering the day has begun . . .
Working hard, the people on tills are tired,
they are shouting 'This till's free!'
Noises of trolleys banging and clanging,
                                        whirling all around.
People moaning, children running all around.
People getting angry.
All the people cramming in the tills
because they want to go home.
Everybody going loading their cars
and putting trolleys back.
Workers shutting the building and the shutters
workers going home gasping for a drink.

Shauna Marcroft (9)
Holy Family RC Primary School

Football Crazy

The players are out and the fans are raging with excitement.
Some fans angry, some fans happy.
Managers shouting, managers singing, some chewing gum.
Some saying 'come on chum,' noise fills the air,
Cheering and jeering, sneezing and coughing, kicking and hitting.
Bashing and trashing with endless rebound . . .
Finally the whistle goes, the players hot, players thirsty,
Fans walk down the stairs, some delighted, some sad,
Cars speed away.
Will they come again?

Cameron Prior (9)
Holy Family RC Primary School

Zoo

The zoo is opening at the start of the day,
Zoo keepers waiting for people to pay,
Walking and talking,
Huffing and puffing,
Moving and pushing,
Twisting around . . .
Spreading around the animals with care.
Crawling and mooching everywhere.
Staring and glaring,
Watching the animals play,
The gates are closing and the cages are
being locked up.
Zoo keepers waiting for people to leave,
Banging and clanging,
Rushing and pushing,
Moving and leaving,
Cars go away.

Laura Abbott (10)
Holy Family RC Primary School

The Safari Theme Park

The safari theme park is quiet,
the animals are hungry,
now they make a lot of noise,
roaring and chirping, hissing and gurgling,
snorting and hooching, moaning and mooching.

The rides are open, it's time to begin,
spinning and twirling, splashing and whirling,
splishing and whizzing, clashing and splashing,
talking and walking, whispering and yelling.

It's time for people to go home,
happy and smiling, hungry and dialling,
laughing and winding, walking and talking,
the day has ended.

Rebecca Winrow (10)
Holy Family RC Primary School

The Zoo

The zoo is silent at the crack of dawn,
Ready for the racket that will follow.
Workers arrive, stuttering into the car park.
The zoo is open, the animals are ready, and the people start to come.
Laughing, chatting and nattering as they see the animals,
The day has begun.

Roaring and clattering as they pass the animals
Crying and shouting, yelling and screaming,
Screeching and shrieking when the animals scare them.
Tamming and cheering, grinning and sneezing
This is a good day.

It's time to go and the people are leaving,
Talking and moaning, grinning and groaning.
The workers are ready to pack up the animals,
Clashing as they shut the cage.
The keepers are hungry, they go to their cars.
Crunching and munching as they eat.
The zoo is peaceful.

Stephanie Marsh (9)
Holy Family RC Primary School

The Stars Haiku

Stars twinkle brightly,
like a torch shining above,
they glow everywhere.

Kirsty Southworth (9)
Holy Family RC Primary School

Sunshine Haiku

Sun shines in the sky,
Like a diamond way up high,
All day long till night.

Rauridh Earley (9)
Holy Family RC Primary School

Fudge My Rabbit Haiku

Fudge, my cute rabbit,
Lies out in the bright sunlight,
Relaxing all day.

Megan Woodcock (9)
Holy Family RC Primary School

Stars Haiku

Stars shining above
Stars flickering in the night
Stars floating about.

Sean Rushe (9)
Holy Family RC Primary School

My Cat

My cat, Keith
Has big teeth
Runs for miles
Falls on tiles
That bear trying to eat his fur
Sticky tongue
Always wrong
Wet nose
Tiny toes.

Paul Hitchen (11)
Lamberhead Green CP School

Racing Car Number Nine

Racing car number nine,
racing down the long track line.
Number ten crashes again,
round the bend, near the end.
Racing through the finish line,
the winner is number nine!

Jordan Hurst (11)
Lamberhead Green CP School

Milkman

My dad is a milkman called Dean
His milk float is a smashing machine
I go with him sometimes
Only when the sun shines
When it is raining I'm never so keen.

Jemma Waite (11)
Lamberhead Green CP School

A Kenning Of A Dog

Tail wagger
Teeth dagger
Howls at night
Teeth that bite
Lots of fur
Like a bear
Wet nose
Tiny toes
Very snuggly
Also cuddly
Chews on bones
Sometimes groans
Runs for miles
Slips on tiles.

Adam Dawber (10)
Lamberhead Green CP School

Kennings Dog

Tail licker
Flea flicker
Fur shaker
Mess maker
Basket sleeper
Night eater
Bum sniffer
Wet kisser
Eye blinker
Water drinker
Angry howler
House prowler.

Tanya Wilkinson (11)
Lamberhead Green CP School

Kennings Dog

Tail wagger
Toy dagger
Sharp jaws
Four paws
Bad hisser
Sloppy kisser
Meat eater
Warm heater
Lap sitter
Ball hitter
Eye blinker
Water drinker
Bone licker
Ball nicker
Anger nipper
Good dipper.

Rebecca Lawton (11)
Lamberhead Green CP School

Kennings Dolphin

High dipper
teeth nipper
water drinker
eye blinker
tail flicker
skin licker
wet kisser
ocean hisser
fish eater
can you guess what it is?

Jade Ingham (11)
Lamberhead Green CP School

Fairy Tale Poems

Peter flies across the sky,
Dorothy sits in the castle and cries,
Aladdin and Jasmine's carpet flies,
Pinocchio's nose grows as he lies.

Goldilocks breaks a chair,
Simon's no money for the fair,
Matilda's mum just doesn't care,
Mufasa and Simba are sleeping in their lair.

Mary Poppins slides up the stairs,
Harry found where Fluffy lurks,
Black Beauty is a beautiful mare,
Winnie the Pooh is a well-loved bear.

Vicky Kay (11)
Lamberhead Green CP School

Kennings Dog

Tail shaking
Din making
Binbag breaking
Newspaper taking
Claw tapping
Paddy taking
Lap sitting
Moon howling
Ball hitting
Cat chasing
Dog food eating
Loveable dog.

Christopher Price (11)
Lamberhead Green CP School

KENNINGS FASHION

Earrings
Hair bobbles
Designer dress
Knees wobble.

Red lipstick
Eye shadow
Beauty Queen
Mirror maddo!

Blonde hair
Nail polish
Lipstick
Eye liner.

Lee Ashurst (11)
Lamberhead Green CP School

MUMS!

Spring cleaner
Grows meaner
High heel wearer
Homework scarer
Tea burner
Shoe buyer
Chip pincher
Loud winger
Couch sitter
Not a-knitter
Hair scruffer
I suffer!

Jessica Stretton (11)
Lamberhead Green CP School

THE KENNING DOG

Tail twister
Bone eater
Cat player
House stayer
Super runner
Fast eater
Wins races
At all places.

Daniel Porter (10)
Lamberhead Green CP School

KENNINGS RABBIT

Tail flicker,
Fur licker,
Foot thumper,
Head bumper,
Bunny hugger,
Food juggler,
Water drinker,
Nose couldn't be pinker!

Bridie Blundell (11)
Lamberhead Green CP School

KENNINGS DOG

Angry barker
Wet kisser
Inside sleeper
Bone chewer
Fierce eater

Teeth nipper
Cat chaser
Fast runner
Ball catcher
Spider killer
Tea drinker.

Kate Watts (10)
Lamberhead Green CP School

Feelings

Feelings are hidden treasures,
locked away inside you and I,
the more you share,
the more you care,
the more friends you can pair.
Feelings are locked and hidden in our body,
so you'll never have chance to say you're sorry.

Amy Smith (10)
Marsh Green Primary School

Hidden Treasures

The gold was in the box
The gold was waiting for some people
to come to count the treasures.
The pirate came to get the treasures.
The pirate took the treasures to the ship.
They opened the box.
There was no treasure in the box.

Georgina Gregory (8)
Marsh Green Primary School

HIDDEN TREASURES

H idden treasures
I nside a box
D own in the ground
D own in the soil
E verywhere there are treasures
N obody knows.

T orn pictures
R ough pictures
E verywhere
A lways been there
S omebody knows
U nderneath the soil they dig
R ound the garden they go
E ven round the street
S sshhh!

Tanya Hilton (10)
Marsh Green Primary School

HIDDEN TREASURES

My pet that is as small as a pea
That's the hidden treasure for me.
My GameBoy that I play on all day
Other people always say
'What stupid things you're just a geek
And don't forget you're a freak.'
My treasures are still good to me
I play with them, they bring me glee.
My best treasures are Mum and Dad,
To have them two I am glad.

Mark Hunter (11)
Marsh Green Primary School

HIDDEN TREASURE

H ey you stop right there
I ’m in the middle of nowhere
D own down someone’s here
D uck, duck I’m full of fear
E very time I try to run
N o stop, this is no fun.

T rying to find some treasure
R ight now it isn’t a pleasure
E verywhere we have been
A hoy! Ahoy! You won’t guess what I’ve been
S orry this treasure is mine
U nique, great we have come to the end of the line
R unning, running with joy
E verybody ahoy! Ahoy!

Jade Clayton (11)
Marsh Green Primary School

HIDDEN TREASURES

Golden box,
Worthless - but full of surprises,
Sit and think nearly all day,
Wondering what lies beneath,
The golden lid.
But I know what really lies beneath it,
Nothing at all.
That’s why
It’s my
Hidden treasures.

Scott Pierce (10)
Marsh Green Primary School

HIDDEN TREASURES

Hidden treasures locked away
I'm going to find them I say
Are they here, are they there?
I'm going to find them anywhere.
The treasures are my toys
They are cuddly they don't make any noise.
They could be in the trees,
And covered beneath the leaves.
They could be on the ground
All around.
Teddy bears
Full of hairs.
They could be in the garden
There are lots and lots of them.

Daniel Holleron (9)
Marsh Green Primary School

HIDDEN TREASURES

Little book full of memories
hidden in my old back garden.
Hidden for two years and eighteen days
in the corner of the garden
next to the old, tall tree.

A book full of notes
a book full of detail
a book full of pictures
all from my ancestors.

Kieron Clough (10)
Marsh Green Primary School

Hidden Treasures

Have a treasure
Keep it safe
Hidden away
In my heart.

Memories
Of me as a baby.
Baby brother being born.

Walking with my grandad,
Bridesmaid at a wedding.

These are my treasures
Of love concealed
In my heart.

Melissa Hudson (10)
Marsh Green Primary School

My Hidden Secrets, Treasure

My world is a big fantasy
Hidden deep in my head
Treasure.

My wish is working with dolphins
Hidden deep in my red-hot, fiery heart.
Treasure.

My heart is full of people who I love
Hidden in my trapped lungs.
Treasure.

Kerry Robinson (11)
Marsh Green Primary School

HIDDEN TREASURES

I have a baby dragon,
in a secret den.
It breathes fire
it's beaten one hundred men.

I have an ancient key
My friends don't know
It leads to a bomb
that doesn't even blow.

I have a helicopter
In a secret base
I can fly anywhere
I can see people race.

I had a robot
that could fly around
I don't like it
because it makes a horrible sound.

David Dootson (9)
Marsh Green Primary School

THE SECRET KEY

My life is a secret,
A secret nobody knows,
My secret is a key,
It will unlock my mother's secret garden,
The garden is my dream,
It's magical forever,
Never I will tell anybody,
This is my life and secret forever.

Natalie Hardman (10)
Marsh Green Primary School

Hidden Treasures

Hidden treasures can be special things,
Like diamonds and ruby rings.
Memories can be in your mind,
The only things you need to find.

Treasures can be lumps of gold,
Or maybe things very old.
Hidden treasures in my mind,
Some are bad and some are kind.

Treasures can be colourful,
Treasures can be very dull.
Treasures can be very bright,
Treasures can reflect the light.

Claire Mahoney (11)
Marsh Green Primary School

My Special Things

My heart is locked away
Hidden deep inside me
Treasure.

Remembering the people I love
Hidden in my feelings
Treasure.

Keeping memories about special books
Hidden in my bedroom
Treasure.

Steven Cornish (10)
Marsh Green Primary School

Hidden Treasures

Hidden treasures can be pleasing,
Rich people are greedy and start teasing.
Most treasures are handled with care,
You may come across some, which are very rare.

Some of my treasures are kept in my head,
A few of them have never been read,
Most of my treasures are:
Memories.

Amelia Whittle (10)
Marsh Green Primary School

The Key To All My Feelings

I have a secret, a secret it may be
The key to all my feelings
A secret just for me.

I have a secret, a secret it may be
My friends are all my feelings
How much they mean to me.
These are my secrets.

Naomi Myers (9)
Marsh Green Primary School

The Doormat Monster

When people come past our doormat
The monster he nicks your teeth
He's a thief and he's a collector
Of what you won't believe

He eats up all your earrings
And he collects the necklaces too
He's a passion for all that's shiny
So watch out, he's after you too!!

Ben Holmes (8)
Parbold Douglas Primary School

Monster Mick

Monster Mick lives in the dump,
He eats people
And metal.
The worst thing he does when he eats,
He goes crunch, slurp,
He munches and worse,
He burps.
He is ugly and cuddly,
But beware, he will eat you.

Daniel Bates (8)
Parbold Douglas Primary School

Little Monster?

He's little and round and likes to poo!
He's never ever used the loo!
He has a nose full of snot.
He only eats food that's hot.
He produces bowls and bowls of wee.
He likes to throw his toys at me.
He bites me and he kicks my mother,
But he's still just my baby brother!

Nicholas Rees (9)
Parbold Douglas Primary School

MONSTER MAD

He's got nails as long as a 30cm ruler
His mouth is as big as a barrel
Filled with potatoes and gravy
His teeth as sharp as a knife
His skin is as scaly as a reptile

He lives in a cave in Mt Everest
It's gooey and ooey in that cave

He scuttles brattles and that's how he moves,
He flies by, never dies
He jumps and bumps

He eats slugs and digs mud
He also eats the children and
You!

Adam Bennett (9)
Parbold Douglas Primary School

THE ALIEN

He has six glaring red eyes
And where his oozing mouth lies,
Are two tongues as thick as a snout,
You better watch out, the alien's about!

He lives on planet Oblong,
He has a son called Bliblong,
The alien lives on thirty rocks,
But he looks nothing like Goldilocks!

Tom Nelson (9)
Parbold Douglas Primary School

The Monster Under My Bed

The monster under the bed
Is enormous, ugly and shy,
It creeps out in the middle of the night,
Weeps and goes back home.

The monster under the bed
Eats all the cheese and nuts,
With his one arm and four legs,
Weeps and goes back home.

The monster under the bed,
He cries because he's alone,
He has no friends of his own,
Weeps and goes back home.

Emma Givens (8)
Parbold Douglas Primary School

Watch Out, It's Coming

Watch out, it's coming to get you
It lives upstairs and munches on pears
It wobbles and gobbles and it wees on the floor
That's a monster for you

All it eats is fingers and toes
It is only just one-year-old
Its teeth are large and very strong
That's my sister for you.

James Ross (8)
Parbold Douglas Primary School

SPIKE

I have a pet monster
He lives in my backyard
He's hairy, big and scary
He is a great house guard

The neighbours don't come near us
They think we're pretty dim
With such sharp teeth and a long, wet nose
They won't make friends with him

It's such a shame, I get the blame
He's such a friend to me
For this pet monster I love to like
He is my dog called Spike!

Kate Nelson (9)
Parbold Douglas Primary School

MONSTER

Monsters are green and red
Monsters live under my bed
Monsters eat garbage and flesh
Monsters hide under my dress

Monsters slip and slither and slurp
Monsters jump and snap and burp
I hate monsters so, so much
I wish he'd stay in his hutch!

Nina Lee (9)
Parbold Douglas Primary School

My Monster

My monster lives under my bed,
When it gets angry it hurts my head.
My monster is my brother,
He acts like no other.

My monster has four eyes,
It flirts with all the other guys.
He eats my clothes
And sucks on lollies loads.

My monster had two noses,
It gulps the water out the hoses.
It has three mouths
And moos like cows.

Victoria Johnston (8)
Parbold Douglas Primary School

The Monster Who Lives Under My Bed

There's a monster that lives in my house,
He lives under my bed.
He eats, he slurps, he gobbles,
He slumps around.

There's a monster that lives in my house,
He lives under my bed.
He squeaks, he squawks, he shuffles, he squeals,
I wish he'd disappear!

Michelle Fox (8)
Parbold Douglas Primary School

THE GOBBAWOK AND ME

The Gobbawok lives under the sea,
You so wouldn't want to live with me.
He slurps and he burps down the meat,
He's got huge, dirty feet.

He swims a lot,
He's covered in blots,
His nose is full of snot,
He's got a funny name that's Chump,
He has got a disease called flump,
His favourite place is the dump,
That's what the Gobbawok does.

So if you ever meet the Gobbawok,
You'd better come with karate chop,
He loves to chase a buzzy bee,
That's the life of the Gobbawok and me.

Sam Ward (9)
Parbold Douglas Primary School

MONKEY MONSTER

Monkey monster lives under my bed
I wish he lived next door instead
He munches and he crunches
He slurps and he burps
I wish I could just go to sleep,
But 'cause of him, I can't!

Stephanie Woods (9)
Parbold Douglas Primary School

SHARK!

There was a big shark,
Swimming underwater in the sea,
His mouth was massive,
His teeth were sharp and pointed,
His eyes were shiny,
His skin was dark and black.

Jonathon Speakman (10)
Rectory CE Primary School

SEASIDE

The calm sea drifts under the clear blue sky.
The volleyball net so wide and so high.
Windsurfing, water skiing, scuba diving too.
Everything you'd want on a holiday to do.
The beach café's great, the beach hut is cool
Then when I've finished, I jump in the pool.

Jordan Roberts (10)
Rectory CE Primary School

SNAIL

Snail,
Slow, slimy,
Hard, shiny, swirly,
Grotesque - leaving a trail!

Emma Hilton (10)
Rectory CE Primary School

THERE'S SOMEONE IN OUR CLASS . . .

There's someone. In our class who. Cannot write.
In sentences, this. Someone never. Listens!
Write in proper sentences!

Their's sumwon in hour classs huw canut spel proplee
this sumwon nevere lisens!
Use a dictionary!

Theressomeoneinourclasswhodoesnotleaveafingerspa
cebetweenhiswordsthissomeoneneverlistens!
Leave a finger space!

There's someone in our class who
writes too big this someone is a very
small person not like his writing!
Write a bit smaller!

There's someone in our class who writes too small this someone
is a very big person unlike his writing!
Write a bit bigger!

There's someone in our class who . . . What was I saying?
Please concentrate!

THERE'S SOMEONE IN OUR CLASS WHO
WRITES IN CAPITAL LETTERS, THIS SOMEONE
NEVER LISTENS!
Use lower case letters!

There's someone in our class who
writes just perfect this someone always
listens!
Very good!

Lindsey Kay (11)
Rectory CE Primary School

KITE

Flying
high in the
light blue sky
with colours of blue,
orange, green and yellow
too. Smooth, long tail
swishing around far
away from the
ground, dancing
in the air.
I wish the
wind was
always
there.
Grasping
the
handle
very
tight
it's
so
fun
I'll
stay
till
night.

Romy Stazicker (11)
Rectory CE Primary School

BENEATH THE WAVES

Beneath the waves is a magical world,
Filled with wonder where the coral is curled.
The brightly coloured fish are all around,
Where even the sharks don't make a sound.
The dolphins bob so quiet, so still
And the huge blue whales hunt for krill.
At night the waves are ready to break
And now the sea is wide awake.
Then comes the fishing boat and down goes the net,
The fish are nearby and the trap is set.
Plenty of creatures come out at night,
It really is a magnificent sight.
At dawn the sun is starting to rise
And the wonderful creatures begin to dive.
Finally, the sun is here at last,
How did this adventure start is what I ask?

Amy Littler (11)
Rectory CE Primary School

THE FAMILY CAR

Some cars are speedy,
Some cars are weedy
And the people that produce them
Are sometimes greedy
The speed is good, the speed is bad
But when it goes wrong
The speed is sad
Maybe it's just a fad
Hope not, I really do!

Daniel Whitehead (9)
Rectory CE Primary School

My Rainbow Poem

Red is for strawberries, so juicy and sweet,
Yellow is for bananas which I love to eat.
Pink is for candyfloss which I buy at the fair,
Green is for the trees that wave in the air.
Orange is for the clothes which I love to wear,
Purple is for the bobbles which I put in my hair.
Blue is for the sky on a lovely summer's day,
This is the end of my poem, I hope you think it's OK!

Katie Lea (9)
Rectory CE Primary School

My Dog

Fast runner
Wet licker
When I run, he runs much quicker
High jumper
Tail thumper
He uses me as his bumper
Soft, silky, furry coat
A little dog is what I quote.

Hannah Lutas (11)
Rectory CE Primary School

What Is A Butterfly?

A butterfly is a fan on the slowest programme.
A butterfly is a leaf fluttering around.
A butterfly is a fairy because it needs dust to fly.
A butterfly is a flying flower.

Natasha Skupski (11)
Rectory CE Primary School

Football

Football, football, it's the best
Better than cricket, better than chess.
I like watching Man U play,
It's a rip-off what you have to pay.
We can beat Liverpool any way,
They're the worst team in the league this day.
I think Ole's good at volleys,
He's a cracker, he can do smackers!

Leigh Taberner (11)
Rectory CE Primary School

In A World Far From Others

Open the door to my dreams.
Look!
A world far from others.
No movement,
No air, no life.
Behold, a new, noiseless planet,
A noiseless world,
A noiseless galaxy,
A noiseless universe.
It is a new, blank sheet
Waiting to be used.
One step,
Two steps,
My footprints imprinted in this enchanted dust.
Now I go
Back to the real world.
Goodbye forever to this new planet . . .
Pars.

Alannah Maggs (10)
R L Hughes Primary School

A Storm

A storm has started,
Heavy rain
Falls like a dripping tap,
Bouncing off the ground
Like on a trampoline.
People scream,
Running around in fear . . .
Thunder!
God is playing skittles up there
Or beating a drum.
Now lasers of bright light
Split the sky,
Like jagged, broken glass
Or daggers stabbing my eyes
Or flickering candles.
They pass in seconds.
A camera?
No lightning dazzling my eyes.
The wind whistles
Like the ref in football.
It rises to a crescendo,
Then sighs.
Black clouds go,
Blue sky appears,
Sunny again,
Red-hot sun beams down,
Very bright,
No storm now,
Everyone is happy, peace has returned.

Katie Smith (10)
R L Hughes Primary School

A New World

Remove the safety lock,
Behold a new mighty generation.
Eyes scan,
Limbs weaken.
Drop,
Slide down the smooth ladder.
Plod,
Thud,
You hit the ground.
Crouch,
Bend,
See a dusty new surface.
Pounce,
Leap,
Like a mighty cat.
I hurdle into the emerald-green sky.
Rolling,
Tumbling,
Falling.
I again catch my balance,
Inspecting every limb.
Rotate!
Spin!
Slowing carefully, begin a second hour journey back.
I've had enough on this planet.

Matthew Birchall (10)
R L Hughes Primary School

ON A NEW PLANET

The flight is over,
Landed
On a new planet.
The door
Bursts open,
Out I go,
Exploring,
A mystery world.
What will I find?
A frog?
Hope not . . . too slimy.
A skeleton?
Hope not . . . too scary.
Look,
A purple star,
How amazing.
Air-can running low!
Air-can running low!
Better go.
Jump
Into the spacecraft,
Zoom off.
Leave behind
The new planet.
Back home I go.

Jack Wheeldin (9)
R L Hughes Primary School

The Storm

Lashing against the houses
Umbrellas inside out
Gushing down the drain
Silver spears thrown down
The rain
Howling like a wolf
Panting and sighing
A tremendous breath
The wind
Bellowing
Angry giants above the clouds
Beat of a drum
Rumbling of a stomach
Such a wonder!
Thunder.

Claire Dean (10)
R L Hughes Primary School

Rainy Days

Rainy days,
Wet days,
Never ever hot days.
Rainy days,
Grey days,
Horrible days,
No play days.
Rainy days,
Never ever dry days.

Rachel Rigby & Rebecca Andrews (8)
R L Hughes Primary School

SPACE

The door screeches open,
I edge down the ladder,
The first person on the moon.
Wonderful!
I trip, the dust rises.
I bounce back up
From the hostile ground,
Higher than a kangaroo,
Over the valleys of dust.
Jump,
Float,
Crash,
Land,
The moon is a beautiful place,
I'll dream of you
From the friendly Earth.

Jade Winstanley (9)
R L Hughes Primary School

RAINY DAYS

Wet, soggy days
Damp, dripping rain
Freezing cold fog
Damp, dull puddles
Rainy days
The misty sky
And dark grey clouds
Everyone stays in
Rainy days.

Claire Lancaster & Hannah Roughley (8)
R L Hughes Primary School

Mystery World

Landing on
An undiscovered world,
Flames, dust,
Wrapping me up,
Blinding my eyesight.
Thud!
Gravity is strong.
Bang!
I hear my foot
Hit
The unyielding surface . . .
The first step.
Spots . . .
Red, yellow, orange,
Volcanoes erupting,
Hot, thirsty,
A mirage in a burning land.
Air,
Purple sky,
Like a painted rainbow,
Drifting
Gently, smoothly like a cloud.
Tiptoe back,
Not a sound
Or you'll wake
The mystery world.

Farima Mehrabi (9)
R L Hughes Primary School

Reflections Of An Evacuee

8am and I'm walking to school,
But I have my suitcase with me,
They say I'm going away,
But where will that be?

I stepped onto the train,
The ride felt cool,
I felt a bit sick
And then started to drool.

I jumped off the train,
They said we were going away,
But where?
They did not say.

I got picked,
But one of the last,
They went slow in the truck
And thought they were going fast.

My new home was rubbish,
But at least I was somewhere,
I was so hungry,
So they gave me a pear.

I was happy at first,
Then I felt upset,
I was missing my family,
But don't forget my pet.

Alexandra Audrey Fairhurst (11)
R L Hughes Primary School

GROWN UP

Having my own job,
Having my own car,
All my studies done,
    Oh, I wonder what it's like
        To be grown up?

Won't wash up for Mum,
Go shopping on my own,
Live in my own house,
    Oh, I wonder what it's like
        To be grown up?

Thoughtful and brave,
So clever I'll be,
My mind will surprise them,
    Oh, I wonder what it's like
        To be grown up?

An imagination so bold,
A job so cool,
No more maths or school,
    Oh, I wonder what it's like
        To be grown up?

When I'm 21, I'll be so happy,
I'll be grown up,
I can't wait for that day,
    Oh, I wonder what it's like
        To be grown up?

My mind will be filled
With laughter and song
And I'll be strong,
    Oh, I want to be grown up.

Laura Collier (10)
R L Hughes Primary School

The Reflections Of An Evacuee

I could feel the excitement
And the joy
We were being so good
They gave us a toy

We had just left
On a very big train
But somewhere deep down
I felt a pain

My brother and I started
To cry
He said
'What if Mummy and Daddy die?'

But now I am
All alone
Clutching the bear
My mummy had sewn

We had just
Left the train
And still
There was that pain

Then a kind lady came
She picked out my brother
But nobody else
Wanted the other

The other was me
I was on my own
Still clutching the bear
My mummy had sewn.

Victoria Clark (11)
R L Hughes Primary School

Magic Planet

Crash!
Here we are
On the mysterious planet.
No food,
No water,
No life.
Wearily I edge down the ladder.
At a single touch,
The ancient sand spreads
Into a footprint.
Hopping along like a kangaroo,
I make mini bridges.
I stop and stare at the soot-black sky,
The shimmering stars glare down at me.
I trip,
Stumble,
Hop back up again,
Like being on a giant trampoline.

Lauren Rosbotham (10)
R L Hughes Primary School

Money

Money is something
We use every day.
Money is something
We give away.

Money is something
To buy toys.
Money is something
For good girls and boys.

Money is something
That you need.
Money is something
You get for good deeds.

Money is something
That you earn.
Money is something
You can turn
Away.

Emma Campbell (9)
R L Hughes Primary School

MY VERY OWN PLANET

Bang,
We have landed.
I step out of my rocket,
The planet was shaped like a star,
It shone brighter than the sun.
As I walked,
I bounced like a football,
Up
And
Down,
Up
And
Down.
It was a cold planet,
I couldn't stay for long,
So I bounced back into the rocket
And set off,
After all, there's no place like home.

Lauren Keegan (10)
R L Hughes Primary School

My World

My world glistens like tiny diamonds,
My world has very clear glass.
No green grass.
My world has tri-coloured roses,
My world has gorgeous posies.
My world has transparent food.
My world has midget pet dogs,
My world has spotted logs.
My world has chat room pens,
My world has green hens.
In my world work does not exist,
In my world we have jade-green mist.
My world is my imagination.

Jade-Leah Koniuszewska (10)
R L Hughes Primary School

The Gale

Last night was incredible,
The old wooden gate was pulled off its rusty hinges.
Bin lids flung off,
Litter roamed the desolate streets.
Slates were removed from garages,
Because of this wrathful wind.
The demented trees thrashed like a wild dance,
The cold wind howled and screamed constantly,
It was like bloodthirsty wolves in the wind.
A yellow full moon could be seen behind revolving clouds.
Terrifying it was.

Alex Bradley (10)
R L Hughes Primary School

Totally New World

Thud!
I've landed in a totally new world.
I see shadows flickering
In the starlight.
The dark, black air
Whistles past.
I step in the forbidden dust.
I collect,
I collect as I walk,
Moon rock . . .
I collect moon rock.
I inch cautiously to the shuttle,
The dust watching my every move.
I fall . . .
Bounce . . .
Rise.
I have completed my mission.

Rebecca Killilea (10)
R L Hughes Primary School

A Stormy Day

A beastly wind is thundering
Through the puny town
Smashing trees with its brutal force
Scattering piles of litter
Breaking windows
Lock your windows
Shut out its mighty howling
Slowly its invincible power dies down.

Kraig Sheedy (9)
R L Hughes Primary School

MILLENNIUM PLANET

Gaze through the window,
To a non-lived in land,
It's an orbiting planet,
Covered in sand.

Jump through the doorway,
Mind your head,
I'm too cold,
It's warmer in bed.

Inch down the ladder,
It's creepy outside,
Maybe an alien
Comes and hides.

Goodbye planet,
I'm flying away,
Maybe planet,
I'll see you someday.

Kathryn Connelly (10)
R L Hughes Primary School

PLANET BLA BLA BLA

As I fall to the floor
Of the undiscovered magical world,
I sink into the field of sand.
Purple tentacles
Reach out from beside me,
My blood turns to ice.
The lilac snakes
Wrap around me
And pull me to safety.

A blob of custard
Gives me some aqua boots.
Wow, it's magic,
Now I can walk on the sinking ground.
Goodbye for now,
I'll keep my boots
And I'll be back another day.

Nikki Molloy (10)
R L Hughes Primary School

Planet RM

Crash,
Bang,
Thump,
I land on an undiscovered world.
I bounce like a bouncy ball,
Up,
Down,
Up,
Down.
I am floating in space,
I am a bird on planet RM.
Crackle,
Crackle,
I am told to go back,
My time is up.
Swoosh,
I am on my way back home,
See you soon,
Goodbye.

Robyn Macdonald (9)
R L Hughes Primary School

ZORK, THE UNKNOWN PLANET

Bang!
Crash!
The airlock swings open,
The planet seems to be black and white,
Like a cow.
What!
It's an egg with three rings round it.
The atmosphere has millions of holes in it,
Just like Swiss cheese.
Suddenly!
Creatures emerge from massive craters.
Life!
Proof of real life.
I think of a name to call it,
I write it on a flag,
Zork!
I name this planet Zork!
As my craft leaves
I wave to all those creatures
Living on Zork.
Goodbye.

Ross Marsden (10)
R L Hughes Primary School

THE GALE

The full moon was hidden behind the mist,
The new gate had been dismantled from its hinges,
Slates slid from the garage roof.
The trees thrashed as the wind rushed through the branches
Crack,
Bang,

Thunder weaved through the night sky,
Trees make a pattern as they clash together.
Clap,
Hailstones lashed at the window.
The moon came into view.
The storm calms, until another day

Keifer Stanier (10)
R L Hughes Primary School

The Planet Of Alien Life!

At last we have landed,
There is a loud
Bang!
Thud!
The airlock swings open
And reveals the truth
Of this orange, forbidden world.
Suddenly I think of
What life there could be . . .
Martians! Or
Aliens!
I leap outside,
There is hardly any gravity.
Splodge!
My first step is a great
Discovery!
As, when I look,
An alien
Lies before me.
I hop back to the ship with the alien,
Back to the real world.

James Taylor (9)
R L Hughes Primary School

BLUE

Blue is the sky,
With clouds so white.
Blue is the sea,
What a wonderful sight.
Blue is a flower,
That grows in the sun.
Blue are the trainers
That help me run.

Blue is a shirt,
I wear when I play.
Blue is my mood,
On a rainy day.
Blue are my eyes,
So clear and bright.
Blue are the birds,
That are out of sight.

Blue are the sapphires,
In my mum's ring.
'Blue' is the band,
I like to hear sing.
Blue is the police,
The boys in blue.
Blue is a whale,
Much bigger than you.

Blue has many friends,
Green, yellow and red.
But blue is the best
It has got to be said.

Thomas Burton (10)
R L Hughes Primary School

REFLECTIONS OF AN EVACUEE

8:30 it was on a miserable morning,
I was feeling very downhearted and sad.
My mum was whinging alongside me
And telling me not to be bad.

The train stopped at school,
Maybe it wasn't so bad after all.
'Give me your bags everybody.'
'We're getting away from this nasty old war.'

I waved goodbye to my mum,
I was happy but I didn't know when.
I came back and the house was demolished,
I might never see her again.

We stopped and collected our bags,
Stepped out and made a big line.
We marched to the great Town Hall,
Where I hoped we'd be able to dine.

Everyone came into the hall,
I was starting to feel a bit sick.
I knew I wasn't a cute one
And I wasn't to be picked quite quick.

This old lady came and took me,
Her house was very fine.
She cuddled me when I was homesick,
She gave me my first sip of wine.

My mum and dad are always with me,
Soon my heart will break in two.
Now and again a tear trickles down,
I love them, I really do.

Lucy Donelan (10)
R L Hughes Primary School

The Witching Hour

The mist swirled down,
The moon shone bright,
Everything was quiet
In the middle of the night.

On the edge of a forest
By a rustic well,
Stood three old witches
Who began a spell.

'A little bit of this,
A little bit of that,
A foot from a frog,
A tooth from a bat.

The tail of a donkey,
The fin of a fish,
Stir them all together
And make the wish.'

The witches sang,
The witches danced,
All night long
They remained in a trance.

But then came the dawn,
With the birds in song,
Gone were the witches . . .
But not for long.

Ryan Dickinson (9)
R L Hughes Primary School

REFLECTIONS OF AN EVACUEE

I walked to school one morning,
All of us had bags.
Some were dressed in rich clothes,
But I was dressed in rags.

We went on a trip that day,
Without our dads or mums.
The steam train was superb,
For a day no hard math sums!

As we stepped onto the platform,
We saw people everywhere.
This was different to the city
And people began to stare.

We stood next to each other,
Feeling very sick.
It had been a bumpy journey
And I was last to be picked.

My new home was like a palace,
There were servants everywhere.
Every morning when I woke up,
One of them brushed my hair.

I missed my mother and father
And when I came home, I cried.
This was because I found out,
In the war, my dad had died.

Sarah Maher (10)
R L Hughes Primary School

The Gale

That night there was a storm
In a terrible rage!
The big, metal gate
Sounded like an animal smashing
Out of its cage.
Litter bins were rolling around
And litter played in a deserted playground.
Slates ripped off a garage roof.
They sounded like a ghost horse
Galloping on the roof.
Trees thrashed as the wind
Sounded like clouds smashing.
A full moon crept
Through the night sky,
As if it was in a cauldron,
Bubbles floating high.

Ian Robinson (10
R L Hughes Primary School

The Gale

The wind had been savage,
Our gates abandoned their hinges.
It had coaxed lids off bins,
So clusters of rubbish was twirling
And whirling round and round!
Slowly slates slapped the ground.
Trees played judo with passing cars,
While flickers of moonlight travelled through clouds,
Shining a gold stream through the sky.

Lauren Cassidy (10)
R L Hughes Primary School

The New World

Landing
Crash!
A new planet,
Sinking sand,
A stream of orange grains.
The black night sky
Covers the Universe with a
Silk,
Shimmering
Sheet.
The rocky surface
Is like a
Floury, white road.
Now it's time to go
To another planet
And a different world.

Rosie Smethurst (10)
R L Hughes Primary School

A Stormy Day

A savage wind destroys houses,
Dainty petals fly away,
Trees are toppling,
Doors are banging,
Slam! Slam! Slam!
Gates are pounding back and forth,
Twigs and leaves invade the town,
Hats are flying,
Chimneys are falling,
Fences are ripped brutally from the ground.

Ben Cunliffe (9)
R L Hughes Primary School

MY OWN MAGIC WORLD

Glittering,
Sparkling,
High above,
A star,
Or is it?
We take a trip,
Past Saturn
And Mars!
We approach
The glittering,
Sparkling star,
Or is it?
Slip,
Slide,
Skid,
We have landed.
Not a star!
An undiscovered crystal,
Icy, glass, transparent world.
It blinds me with its beauty.
We have to leave my tiny planet,
We'll be back to find new wonders!

Bethany Fulton (9)
R L Hughes Primary School

RAINY DAYS

Rainy days are soggy
And wet
The pipes are flooding
With water
Children splashing in
The puddles.

The shapes go round
And round
The rain falls on
The rooftops
And it goes splat
On windows
I love rainy days.

Lauren O'Neill & Stephanie Beatty (8)
R L Hughes Primary School

Zork

As I leap out of Lex 2000
I stumble,
Trip,
Leap.
The door
Squeaks . . .
Louder,
Slams shut.
I see a new world.
The jet-black sky is blacker than a witch's cat
And the beam of the stars pierces my skin.
As I step I shatter the deep, still silence.
The truth of the planets is here.
I plunge my flag,
It goes deep,
Deeper,
Firmer
Into the murky dust.
I will call this planet Zork.

Adam Carlyle (9)
R L Hughes Primary School

REFLECTIONS OF AN EVACUEE

I was at school playing,
Then this boy ran over to me,
'Sorry,' he said,
'I've just heard you're an evacuee.'

Still angry and upset,
I pile onto the train,
I see my parents crying,
How would they know my pain?

The train ride was brilliant,
I had so much fun.
As I got off the train,
I was blinded by the sun.

We were led into a hall,
Waiting for a couple to see
If they had made the right decision
By choosing me.

Finally I have been chosen,
I am led into her home.
'Don't be lazy!' she yelled,
'Give the dog a bone.'

Day and night I have to work,
Without any breaks.
When I return home,
Mum will see she made a mistake.

Lauren Eaves (10)
R L Hughes Primary School

LATE!

Walked up the drive,
Car murmured, 'Put some tunes on.'
'Can't,' I said. 'Late.'
Got into work,
Lift hummed, 'Top floor mate?'
'Can't,' I said. 'Late.'
Sat at my desk,
Computer beeped, 'Surf the web?'
'Can't,' I said. 'Late.'
Got out lunch,
Sandwich crunched, 'Eat me too?'
'Can't,' I said. 'Late.'
Went back to desk,
File rattled, 'Read me, read me!'
'Can't,' I said. 'Late.'
On my way home,
Keys jingled, 'Lock all the doors.'
'Can't,' I said. 'Late.'
Having my lunch,
Microwave pinged, 'Cook some pizza.'
'Can't,' I said. 'Late.'
Went back to bed,
Bed twanged, 'Please stay in.'
'Can't,' I said. 'Late.'

Damian Hughes (10)
R L Hughes Primary School

My Little Brother

My brother likes to dance
My brother likes to sing
My brother likes to do almost everything
He might play with a ball
Or splash in the bath
But whatever he is doing
He will always have a laugh!

My brother likes to play
My brother is a pain
My brother is totally, utterly insane
He might go to McDonald's
Or watch Winnie the Pooh
And fill his sister's trainers full of green, sticky goo

My brother likes to draw
My brother is aged three
My brother rode his bicycle
But fell and cut his knee
He might mess up my room
Or draw upon my wall
But he is still my little brother
The best one of all.

Charlotte Mason (10)
St Aidan's RC Primary School

Pigs!

Pigs can dance,
Pigs can sing,
Pigs can do almost anything!

Pigs can hide,
Pigs can seek,
Pigs are mild and some are meek!

Pigs are fat,
Pigs are thin,
Pigs that squeal make all the din!

Pigs live in fields,
Pigs live on farms,
Pigs taste best in bacon barms!

Amy Dove (10)
St Aidan's RC Primary School

I Can't Write A Poem

I can't write a poem,
It's just too hard,
What shall I do?
I've got a blank card.

I can't write a poem,
How will I cope?
To see what's on this card,
You'll need a microscope.

I can't write a poem,
Help me please,
I'm scratching myself,
Like I've got fleas.

Wait a minute . . .

I've just written a poem,
Look at my card,
It only took me two minutes
And it wasn't hard.

Emma Rigby (11)
St Aidan's RC Primary School

I CAN'T WRITE A POEM!

I can't write a poem,
I just don't know how,
I can't write a poem,
I think I'll give up now!

I can't write a poem,
I'll bet you all my money,
I can't write a poem
And I don't think it's funny!

I can't write a poem,
I'll tell you that for sure,
I can't write a poem,
I'll need your advice and more.

I've just written a poem!
It just takes some thought!
I've just written a poem!
Thanks for the advice you brought!

I can write a poem!
I'll easily show you how!
I can write a poem!
It seems so simple now!

I can write a poem!
I think I'll celebrate!
I can write a poem!
What do you mean, I finished late!

Joshua Millar (10)
St Aidan's RC Primary School

I'M JUST A LITTLE, UGLY BEAR!

I'm just a little, ugly bear,
My friends have all gone to a loving home
And I'm pushed to one side all on my own,
I'm just a little, ugly bear!

I know I'd be good at giving cuddles and hugs,
But nobody will give me a chance and it really bugs,
I'm just a little, ugly bear!

People don't realise but I have feelings too,
I don't like being thrown about, would you?
I'm just a little ugly bear!

I sometimes dream about being loved by a child,
For me this is just my imagination going wild,
I'm just a little, ugly bear!

My time has come, it's not a dream,
A boy called Joe wants me it seems,
Perhaps I'm not such a little, ugly bear!

Katie Brennan (10)
St Aidan's RC Primary School

RIVERS

The river runs down the valley,
She dresses herself in fish's garments
And swims around the winding country path,
She never gets tired and she never stops
Running.

Lucy Hayes (11)
St Aidan's RC Primary School

My Family

My family are very special
They mean the world to me
There's Mum, Dad and two brothers
And we live together happily

My mum is my best friend
And she always fills my tum
She always makes me happy
Whenever I feel glum

My dad gives me my spend
To buy the things I like
I'm looking forward to my birthday
Because he's buying me a bike

My brothers are older than I am
And they always torment me
But I know they love me really
And I love my family.

Maria Hewitt (10)
St Aidan's RC Primary School

The Witch

The witch will
Fly from the midnight sky,
She'll land in a field,
Silent and quick,
She may look really smart,
But really she's dead thick!

Her potions bubble bright,
So they brighten up the night,
She flies away with a wicked cackle,
With her knees rattling away!
Rattle! Rattle! Rattle!

James Luke Pallister (10)
St Aidan's RC Primary School

Yo-Yos

Yo-yos spin and twist and twirl,
Yo-yos for a boy, yo-yos for a girl.
You can have fun all through the day
But the teachers say, 'Put those yo-yos away.'
One day I went to school
And oops-a-daisy broke the rule,
I took my yo-yo out of my tray
And had to stay in all dinner play.
I kicked, I wailed, I screamed, I cried
Until the teacher let me go outside.

Leanne Jade Hawkins (10)
St Aidan's RC Primary School

Shell Poem

Oval limpets cling,
Spiral dog whelks twist like pasta
Fan-shaped scallops smooth like kittens
On the craggy rocks
In a slimy pool
In dark, gloomy caves.

Joshua Banks (8)
St Mary's Birchley RC Primary School

In A Moment Of Silence

In a moment of silence in Australia,
I heard my Auntie Audrey say, 'G'day mate' to me.

In a moment of silence in Greece,
I heard my footsteps brushing the sunburnt sand.

In a moment of silence in Italy,
I heard the sound of pepperoni pizzas being cooked.

In a moment of silence in the Lake District,
I heard sheep sobbing slightly.

In a moment of silence in Spain,
I heard the soft brushing on a painting by Bartholomé Murillo.

In a moment of silence in France,
I heard someone sipping white wine.

Emily Jayne Veivers (9)
St Mary's Birchley RC Primary School

Inside My Marble

I can see red-hot fire breathing embering flares.
I can see vicious burning fire breathing dragons.
I can see a multicoloured hot firework.
I can see hot smoke coming out of a building.
I can see a tall vampire with fangs down to his knees, 20 eyes
and wings.
I can see a brilliant star planet with billions of bright light stars.
I can see a flying light green car.
I can see a dirty old smelly troll.
I would love to live in my marble, it's incredible.

Hannah Simpson (8)
St Mary's Birchley RC Primary School

Excuses For Forgetting My Homework

I've left it in the bathroom, Sir
Next to our dirty, old bath
Honest, I really have, Sir
Please, try not to laugh

Left it in the town centre, Sir
I was looking at a pen
A three-year-old took it off me, Sir
And ran off there and then

The dog snatched it off me, Sir
And gave me back his bone
Honest, the dog did, Sir
And took it to the Millennium Dome

We got kicked out of our home, Sir
We have to live on the street
Please, believe me, Sir
We had nothing to eat.

Katerina Serefoglou (9)
St Mary's Birchley RC Primary School

Dreaming Is Like . . .

Dreaming is like floating to another world
Dreaming is like flying and never coming down
Dreaming is like being a brand new person
Dreaming is like smelling a brand new smell
Dreaming is like a fresh flower opening
Dreaming is like fresh, beautiful water
Dreaming is like a baby being born
Dreaming is like banging in a goal for Liverpool.

Robert Allen (8)
St Mary's Birchley RC Primary School

SEASHELL

Oval limpets cling
Spiral dog whelks twist
Fan-shaped scallops shine like the moon
On craggy rocks,
In rough, rocky pools
In shadowy, slimy, spooky caves

The foamy, glossy waves wash up sparkling shells
Onto the hot, blasting beach

The shiny, glossy dolphins round up smooth shells
That drop to the crinkly ocean floor

The slimy, green seaweed that grows on the cold ocean bottom
Hide shells of all kinds in their green, tangled leaves.

Jenna Pate (8)
St Mary's Birchley RC Primary School

INSIDE MY MARBLE

I can see
A dinosaur miaowing very loudly.
I can see
A tiny dog breathing flamy fire.
I can see
Me holding the Premiership Cup for Liverpool.
I can see
People racing around like lunatics.
I can see
Dogs buying yards of chocolate from the shops.
I can see
Giant pencils sharpening tidgy people.
I would love to go inside my marble, would you?

Arron Martindale (8)
St Mary's Birchley RC Primary School

Inside My Marble

I can see an erupting volcano
spewing out a river of lava.

I can see mountains of delicious,
cold ice cream.

I can see a monstrous
fire breathing dragon.

I can see huge hills
covered in freezing snow.

I can see me being the captain
of England and lifting the World Cup.

I can see me flying in the blue sky
with all the birds.

Philip Hamnett (8)
St Mary's Birchley RC Primary School

Isuzu Trooper

Isuzu Trooper, four-wheel drive
Turn the key, it comes alive
Down the country lanes we go
Singing songs that we all know
Dad drives this way, then drives that
Mum just sits and has a chat
Grandad Keith and Grandad Bill
Are in the pub upon the hill
Gran and Nanna, they must be
In the café drinking tea
We all meet up and have our dinner
It's a race and I'm the winner.

Amy Kelly (9)
St Mary's Birchley RC Primary School

Dreaming Is Like . . .

Dreaming is like eating and never getting full up.
Dreaming is like your own world.
Dreaming is like breathing underwater.
Dreaming is like sleeping on a cloud.
Dreaming is like long, hot summer days.
Dreaming is like relaxing in my bed.
Dreaming is like an adventure for eternity.

Elizabeth Hague (9)
St Mary's Birchley RC Primary School

In A Moment Of Silence

In a moment of silence I heard the pitter-patter of the rain
In a moment of silence I heard the zip zip of a pencil case
In a moment of silence I heard the click click of a computer
In a moment of silence I heard the clang clang of a chair moving
In a moment of silence I heard the rattle rattle of some papers
In a moment of silence I heard the bang bang of books being
dropped on the table.

Rachel Fletcher (8)
St Mary's Birchley RC Primary School

Horses

Stable keepers
Hay eaters
Noise makers
Long trotters
Quick walkers
No talkers

Show jumpers
Loud trumpers
Apple snatchers
No good catchers.

Laura Kirby (11)
St Mary's Birchley RC Primary School

War

I sat on the floor, torn apart
This is the war that had broken my heart
The darkness came
And so had the rain
I scrambled to the old rickety train
Crying and crying and dying in pain
My life has been nothing but a shame.

Christopher Fleming (11)
St Mary's Birchley RC Primary School

Dreaming

Dreaming is like falling into a tub of flowers
Dreaming is like diving into a cold swimming pool
Dreaming is like racing cars in the Grand Prix
Dreaming is like walking into a land called Neverland
Dreaming is like swimming in a pool of flowers
Dreaming is like running in the Olympic Games
Dreaming is like winning on sports day.

Robert Caddock (8)
St Mary's Birchley RC Primary School

THE WRITER OF THIS POEM

The writer of this poem is
As quick as can be
As clever as an owl
As sturdy as a tree
As sharp as a pencil
As long as a stick
As clean as a dentist
As quick as a tick
As wriggly as a worm
As long as a snake
As happy as a clown
As beautiful as a lake
The writer of this poem
Is a really good mate
The writer of this poem
Is called Cait.

Caitlin Thompson (10)
St Mary's Birchley RC Primary School

DAYDREAMS

Mr Barnes thinks I am working although I am not there,
I'm in a big, big world of dreams, I'm zooming through the air,
Surrounded by white puffy clouds, selling ice cream to the stars,
Travelling higher through the sky, destination Mars,
Green and yellow marshmallows whirling through the sky,
Clouds that look like clowns make me laugh until I cry,
Strawberry sauce is dripping, sticking to my feet,
It's making me real hungry, I really need to eat,
Suddenly it starts to rain and sherbet's falling fast,
My daydream's nearly over, it was far too good to last.

Shaunna Kerr (11)
St Mary's Birchley RC Primary School

Sounds

My sister's eerie scream
My brother's shrieking yell
The sound of a crackling fire
The rusty old school bell
The boiling of the kettle
The brewing of the tea
The breaking of the biscuits
Most of them for me

These sounds are very queer
In other people's homes
With Mum and Dad going mad
And talking garden gnomes
At night all is silent
All silent in the night
All is dark and quiet
There isn't a tiny glimpse of light.

Rachel Frackelton (10)
St Mary's Birchley RC Primary School

Inside My Marble

I can see India covered in Indians.
I can see a gloomy, misty, violet planet.
I can see a shooting star heading for Mars.
I can see hot, streaming lava heading to a city.
I can see Egypt covered in grape juice.
'Mum, can I go in my marble?'
'Yes, but be back for tea.'
'Yes Mum, N O spells, no.'

George Cullen (8)
St Mary's Birchley RC Primary School

Spells For My Teacher

1 bottle of vodka
2 crates of brew
Make my teacher
Go down the loo

3 squeaky grey rats
1 big red van
Make my teacher
Turn into a man

1 large red lamp
1 bottle of fizzy Fanta
Make my teacher
Turn into Santa

3 fierce bats
5 bottles of beer
Make my teacher
Look like Edward Lear

1 screaming zombie
1 big giant log
Make my teacher
Turn into a frog

2 bottles of water
1 piece of coal
Make my teacher
Turn into a mole.

Michael Jones (9)
St Mary's Birchley RC Primary School

The Universe

Star
Star
Shining
Bright

Shining
In the
Freezing
Night

Shining
Big
Shining
Small

I really
Hope
You
Do
Not
Fall

The moon
The moon
Shining like a silver spoon
Sometimes red, sometimes white
Always giving a night-time light
The moon
The moon
The moon.

Dominic Morris (10)
St Mary's Birchley RC Primary School

New House

We moved into our new house two weeks on Wednesday,
That's where we live and we're going to stay.

It was okay at first,
But then our bathroom pipe burst.

The entire bathroom was full of water
And that was only for starters.

Next door at night made lots of noise,
So we were up all night playing with our toys.

One night Mum got really angry,
So she went next door to Mr and Mrs Langy.

As soon as they opened the door, Mum started shouting at them,
All they could say was 'A way a hey hey, it's the lady from number 10.'

This made Mum even more mad,
I started wondering why is this house so bad?

It got even worse,
It was like our house was under a curse.

Drunken men coming from the pub across the road,
Saying that they had had one when they had had a load.

So here we are with our bags packed once again,
Never to return to Lodge Road, number 10.

Emily Collins (10)
St Mary's Birchley RC Primary School

Excuses For Forgetting My Homework

It burnt to a crisp, Sir,
When I left it near the boiler.
I tried to get rid of the fire, Sir,
So I rinsed it in the toilet.

I left it at the zoo, Sir,
They said it tasted nice.
I mean the fierce lions, Sir,
They ate it with fried mice.

Our house was knocked down, Sir
And I left the work inside.
It wasn't supposed to be our house, Sir,
But the one on the other side.

I was walking off to school with it, Sir
And stopped to tie my lace.
I left it on a bin, Sir
And the bin men I tried to race.

I accidentally blew it up, Sir
And I was seeing stars.
It was a very loud bang, Sir,
You could hear it on Mars.

Patrick Preston (10)
St Mary's Birchley RC Primary School

THE BOY WHO GOT TIED UP IN A SACK

This is a boy called Jack
Who accidentally got tied up in a sack
He punched and kicked and tried to get out
And he yelled and screamed and gave a big shout
He tried and tried to open the knot
He had to stop because he was too hot

The air got thinner until he couldn't breathe
Then thankfully along came his best friend, Steve
Who heard Jack scream and grunt and shout
For goodness sake, can you get me out!

Jack said, 'Hurry you'd better be quick
For I am going to be awfully sick'
So Steve quickly opened the tightened knot
And Jack said, 'At last, thanks a lot.'

John Bostock (9)
St Mary's Birchley RC Primary School

I DETEST SCHOOL!

I detest school!
Everyone thinks it's cool.
I would rather spend the day in a swimming pool.
All the teachers said, 'Copy out the school rules.'
I hate my horrible school.
My friend said, 'Don't be a fool and run away from school.'
But it used to be so cool,
Till one dinner time, I disobeyed the rules
And I had to write out 50 times, 'I must obey the school rules'
And that is why I hate school.

Christopher Mee (11)
Sacred Heart RC Primary School

The Lost City Of Atlantis

Hidden treasures, where are they?
Waiting for that perfect day,
When special people come and find
Lots of gold of different kinds,
As deep sea divers often miss
The city of Atlantis!

The radiant towers as tall as can be,
Making it hard for the people to see,
The bodies and buildings peacefully lie,
As the souls of its people go slowly on by.

The lost city's possessions are long in the past,
The solemn remembrance is just sure to last.

Catherine Gallagher (11)
Sacred Heart RC Primary School

My Hidden Treasure

I played in the countryside every day
Where the beautiful green grass lay
I climbed a tall hill
Where there stood a windmill
I saw the dimpling river pass
And be the sky's blue looking-glass
The dusty roads go up and down
With people trampling into town
As the sun went down
I saw the people come out of town
As it was the end of the day
I would just like to say
That this is my treasure
And will be forever.

Ashleigh Crockett (10)
Sacred Heart RC Primary School

HIDDEN TREASURES

A cow has its udders,
A lion has its mane,
A horse has agility,
A cut well, has pain.

Stories have endings,
Greek men have myths,
Rivers have their ripples,
Mountains have their cliffs.

Jails have their criminals,
Bread has its crust,
Mansions have vast hallways,
Our houses, they have us.

The world has its horizon,
The sky has its sun,
My treasure is hidden,
Guess what? It's my mum.

Darrell Unsworth (11)
Sacred Heart RC Primary School

BABA BEN

Baba Ben needs a pen
He'll cry and cry until he's dry
He'll scream and scream
Until he gets mean
He'll smack his mum
If he gets a hungry tum
His mum said, 'OK'
He shouted out, 'Yippee'
His mum said, 'Let's go up Leigh.'

Nathan Hughes (8)
Sacred Heart RC Primary School

My Friend

My friend is lively all the time
We're having a sleep-over
We go to bed at nine
Here comes the morning
We are talking
While we are walking

Her bedroom is fresh
And a mess
After Mum shouted us down
For tea, it was chicken crown
After tea we went outside
She said a joke to me
Here comes the funny line

We had a laugh
Then a splash in the bath
We had sometime to knit
Then the fire lit
My mum came to pick me up
So I shouted 'Bye.'

Emily Hesketh (8)
Sacred Heart RC Primary School

Mysterious House

One night I had a fright,
I decided to look through my window
And so I got dressed and looked my best.
I went down the curved stairs,
I opened the door and before I knew,
I was at the house,
Still as quiet as a mouse.

Rebecca Dainty (11)
Sacred Heart RC Primary School

HIDDEN TREASURES

Gold is a treasure
But not like my treasure
They rattle your brains
And put knowledge in your head
They make you remember numbers
And talk about the books you've read
They teach you how to spell
To write plays and myths
They teach you everything
To make you learn and earn
You learn about Jesus
With these special creatures
But if it wasn't for God
These creatures called teachers
Would not teach us.

Phillip Gibson (9)
Sacred Heart RC Primary School

HIDDEN TREASURE IS NEAR ME

When I was born, I found my true treasure
They looked after me
And loved me
They are kind and loving
And both of them are generous.

They are always there for me
When I am sad or lonely
They shout at me when I jump upstairs
But it is not the end of the world
But at the end of the day
They are Mum and Dad.

Natalie Williams (10)
Sacred Heart RC Primary School

SWEETIE LAND

Lollies hanging from the trees,
Bubblegum on strings.
Daises you can eat,
Lots of little things.

Rainbow drops, minty grass,
Gummy bears and candy sticks!
Buttercups and creamy mushrooms,
Chocolate river, pick and mix.

Sweetie land is loads of fun,
It really is a pleasure.
In my dreams I go right there,
Shh, it's my hidden treasure!

Megan Hayes (10)
Sacred Heart RC Primary School

MY SPECIAL TREASURE

She is pretty and glittery
And is very witty
She hugs me and kisses me
And flows like the sea

She is very nice
And doesn't like spice

She is very caring
And sharing
And she is very special
She is my treasure
Because she is my mum.

Lindsey Geraghty (10)
Sacred Heart RC Primary School

Friends

I have a special friend
A very special friend
Her name is Hayley
And she really is a special friend

This special friend of mine
Is lovely and energetic
She really loves to dance and sing

I don't like to sing but I really like to dance
That's why she's my really special friend

We play lots of good games
My special friend and me
She is so generous
I love her to bits
My special friend and me.

Sara Fowler (10)
Sacred Heart RC Primary School

My Special Treasure

Ten years ago I found my hidden treasure,
She is kind and helpful
And is always there for me,
I really love my hidden treasure,
It's hidden close to me,
She makes my tea and does everything for me,
As my hidden treasure loves me too,
Because my hidden treasure is my mum.

Cloey Seddon (10)
Sacred Heart RC Primary School

Angels

I believe in angels
The people in the sky
They walk beside us
Always guide us
All of our lives

I believe in angels
They're always there with me
To help me through
When times get rough
And I don't know what to do

I believe in angels
They're such special things
They are hidden treasures
That will never melt away.

Amy Burdon (10)
Sacred Heart RC Primary School

My Hidden Treasure

In my dream world is where I'll stay,
Hour after hour, day after day,
Where the clouds are made from candyfloss,
Where chocolate frogs and billy goats cross,
So this is where I'd like to be,
Where no one in the world can see,
In my dream world full of feathers
And also all my hidden treasures.

Natasha Wild (10)
Sacred Heart RC Primary School

A Perfect Dream

Dreams are lots of pictures
Full of different moving figures
Swimming all around in your head
Whilst you're snoring away in bed
Candyfloss or maybe chocolate
Will be some you'll never forget
Toffee trees and sugar clouds
Voices screaming really loud
Chocolate soil and fudge as stones
Chat for hours on furry phones
Shopping for clothes and playing games
Ending the day by painting frames
No work, more play, I'm very keen
Wouldn't that be the perfect dream?

Zoe Jackson (11)
Sacred Heart RC Primary School

My Special Friend

My special friend never tells a lie
He's always kind and he'll sometimes stay outside
He's sometimes asleep, he's sometimes awake
He won't make a noise and he doesn't live in a lake
When I lie in bed at night, I wonder what he's thinking
Is it a racing car or probably a ship sinking?
My best friends have best friends
But I stick to my very best friend
Smokey, the guinea pig.

Nichola Hunt (10)
Sacred Heart RC Primary School

My Special Animal

My treasure is my dog, my dog is there
When I am sad and lonely.
I cuddle my dog, she makes me happy.

She is called a chow-chow, a big fluffy dog,
She would not hurt a fly, my dog is gentle
And caring.

There is no animal that could be like my dog, Nala,
I think she is very special to me,
Even though she is just a dog.

I do not care what they will say about my dog,
She is always a
Treasure to me.

Jordon Dawes (10)
Sacred Heart RC Primary School

Why?

Why do I never get to pick who's on?
Why is everyone faster than me?
Why does everyone make fun of me?
Why do people think they're better than me?
Why is it always my fault?
Why was I the son with haemophilia?
Why did my dad leave me and Mum?
Why is life unfair?
Do you know I never knew there were so many questions in life.
I always thought there wasn't a lot of questions in life,
But now I see that there are a lot of questions in life.

Rhys Gillingham (9)
Sacred Heart RC Primary School

Shadows In The Night

Shadows in the night,
Moving at great speed,
Everything dark, not bright,
Switching shapes as they please.

All is still and silent,
A bit spooky in a way,
The mirror on the wall so shiny,
As if it was cleaned today.

A strange atmosphere surrounded me
And sent a shiver down my spine,
My face dropped, dropped sharply,
As if I was lost in time.

Martin Rawsthorne (11)
Sacred Heart RC Primary School

My Dream

Dreams are small pictures
Dancing in your head,
Won't it be the perfect dream
If it goes something like this?
Chocolate swirls as flowers,
Candyfloss as clouds,
Orange are the rivers,
Biscuits for the bark,
Nougat for the grass,
Toffee as the paths that lead
To the white chocolate walls,
That would be the perfect dream,
Until your alarm goes *ding!*

Hayley Coates (11)
Sacred Heart RC Primary School

My Dream Treasure

My treasure is not my cat.
My treasure is not my brother
And my treasure is not my dad.
It might be my sister,
But it might be my fish.
I'm coming closer
And closer,
But I'm not coming closer.
It might be my dog
And I've hid it.
It begins with M,
I think someone has found it,
It is my special mum.

Megan Williams (10)
Sacred Heart RC Primary School

Me And My Sisters

Gillian, my sister
Is only thirteen,
She is in year nine
And she never looks clean.

Gail, my older sister
Is the best,
She is very tall
And she is the best of the rest.

Well, now you know my sisters
And they're a pleasure, I think you know
That they're my treasure.

Steven Unsworth (9)
Sacred Heart RC Primary School

DOLPHINS

They splish and they splash
They curve and they dash
As the turquoise waves bash

Fins racing hard
To keep pace with the boats
They flash off the coasts

They hunt for their food
In the reflection of the shining moon.

Charlotte Heaton (10)
Sacred Heart RC Primary School

MY TREASURES

My treasure is not sweets
My treasure is not honey
My treasure is not food
My treasure is not fun
My treasure is not home
My treasure is my friends and my family.

Rachel Chapman (9)
Sacred Heart RC Primary School

HIDDEN TREASURE

There's treasure in the sky,
Treasure nearby,
Where the birds fly
And fish swim.

Wherever you go,
There are always treasures,
For different people there are different treasures,
My treasure is my mum and dad.

James Stott (10)
Sacred Heart RC Primary School

SWIMMING

Swimming front, swimming back
Fly and breast are the best
Dive and jump in the air
Whirl and twirl everywhere
Under, over, in and out
Moving all about
Swimming here, swimming there
Swimming everywhere.

Emma Lees (11)
Sacred Heart RC Primary School

OUR PLAYGROUND

Our playground is jet-black
With cobwebs in the corners
And in-between the cracks

And with the sunrise
The cobwebs shine and glitter
All around the playground.

Rebecca Gill (11)
Sacred Heart RC Primary School

Miss Mable

I'll tell you about
My teacher, Miss Mable
Who ate the chairs
And the table
She ate all the books
And the toy ducks
Our teacher, Miss Mable

But one day was particularly weird
She came into school
And had grown a beard
We asked her why
She did reply
It was to catch
The leftovers from her meal

When the bell rang
We came into class
And found Miss Mable
Guzzling the grass
She had eaten the field
And the fence shield
We had to drag her
Back to class

Now she's grown
To 35 stone
And on a diet
To eat only bones
Bu the worst thing is
Now brace yourself!
She burst yesterday
And is on a McDonald's shelf!

Corrina Connor (10)
Sacred Heart RC Primary School

My Treasure

My treasure isn't gold,
My treasure isn't money,
My treasure isn't sugar,
My treasure isn't honey.

My treasure isn't pasta,
My treasure isn't pizza,
My treasure isn't turkey,
My treasure isn't chicken tikka.

My treasure isn't my bed,
My treasure isn't my pillow,
My treasure isn't my teddy,
My treasure isn't willow.

My treasure is my mum.

Matthew Jarram (9)
Sacred Heart RC Primary School

A Treasure That Nobody Knows

Some people say that treasures are
jewels in the sea.
Some people say that treasures are
friends and family.
Some people say that treasures are
their thoughts and their dreams.
But I say that treasures are
gifts, talents and more.
My favourite treasure is writing poems,
poems galore.

Hayley Unsworth (10)
Sacred Heart RC Primary School

TREASURE

Deep down in the oceans of Greece,
There lies hidden treasure,
It's not gold,
Not jewellery,
But love and care.
This has not been spread,
But there is a way
And that is to show
Evil people like terrorists and robbers,
Their kind of treasure
Is hatred and greed.
But if only they
Had sparkling treasure,
The world would be a better place.

James Cooper (10)
Shevington CP School

MY LOCKET

My locket is so special to me,
I wear it every day as you can see.
It's in the shape of a heart
And it's as silvery as the moon!
Inside there's a picture of my friend,
Our friendship will never end.
It has a sparkling chain
And it's my magical treasure!
It's kept in my wooden box,
I lock it up with my silver lock.
It's my own special secret,
My locket is so special to me!

Emma Louise Hall (10)
Shevington CP School

Friendship Is A Journey

Secrets for only friends to know,
Dreams to be told.
Let's go in my mind
To find some more.
As quick as a flick
You're in my mind,
Look deep and hard,
You've found them.
Treasures of laughter
Locked in a box,
Treasures of deep, dark friendship
To be shared.
Now come out my mind,
You know the poem of friendship,
So you can be my
Friend.

Hannah Temple (10)
Shevington CP School

My Pal, Steven

My pal, Steven is very nice,
He can be naughty or good, it's a roll of the dice,
Compared to him the strongest men are mice.
He is wicked and very cool
And is never a fool.
He is absolutely the best
And a lot better than the rest.
He is super hip
And is so strong he can lift up a ship.
Overall he's a dead nice bloke
And his favourite drink is definitely Coke!

Matthew Galloway (11)
Shevington CP School

THE NIGHT MAN

Once every night,
The night man comes.

He walks silently through the street,
Like a bird on its prey.

The only light the street has
Are his eyes.

Like a torch,
Attached to him everywhere he goes.

His breath is like the wind,
Breathing softly in the air.

Knocks on my window,
Like a ghost haunting me!

Fingers like ice,
Moves everywhere he goes.

He sits silently,
In a weak silent pose.

Louise Boardman (10)
Shevington CP School

A SNAKE

Their eyes are like a great big green sun.
They slither along like a little worm underground.
They rattle like some beads in a tube.
Their tongue is like a barbeque fork with the revolting spit coming out.
They shed their skin then it falls down their sandpapery back.
Their mouth is like a rock cave.

Christopher Lyon (10)
Shevington CP School

THE SPARKLING BOX

I will put in my box
The sparkling leotard that won me a gold
The pose like a star up in the sky
A wish like a holiday in Spain or Las Vegas
A hug from Britney and a mouthful of ice cream
I will put in my box
The swish of my bridesmaid dress
And a glimpse of a diamond up in the sky
I will put in my box
Icing diving down into the deep soft doughnut
And Dot the dinosaur driving the dinky mobile
My box is made out of soft tasty icing
And creamy caramel on the top
Diamonds and rubies for the hinges
A sparkling star on the top, gleaming in the sky
I will surf on a cloud
And dive into a doughnut
I will jump into the dinky mobile
But . . . most of all I will stuff my face with . . .
Ice cream.

Katie Davies (10)
Shevington CP School

THE CARING BOX

I will put in my box,
The feeling of friendship.
The smell of a rose in a garden.
The taste of soup trickling down my throat.
The sound of smacks on the mats in jujitsu.
The sight of motocross bikes racing to the track.
The touch of fur on top of a cat's head.

Oliver Davies (9)
Shevington CP School

THE DUMP

Engine oil,
Chocolate foil,
Bent metal,
An old rusty kettle,
Lots of wood,
Horrid old food,
A huge crane,
A little toy train,
A tiny toy car,
A puddle of tar,
A worn out rope
And a broken bike slope,
Smelly old bins,
Lots of sharp pins,
Broken plates,
A pile of slates,
I haven't been there for years and years,
But I know there are paintings of wild deers.

Kier James Willetts (10)
Shevington CP School

HIDDEN PLACES

My hidden place is my tree house,
No one but me can get in, not even a mouse.
It is so cool, I play there all day,
Until I go away.
I will come back the next day I say,
The next day comes around to a sad day.
The wind had come around and around
And the tree came down and down.
My hidden treasure was now gone.

Jake Howard (11)
Shevington CP School

The Night

The night
It gives me a fright
There are shadows
Noises
Flap flap
What was that?
It's a bat
I dive under my covers
Like a super diver
I close my eyes
I can see white dots
They're like little flies
I wait
And wait
And wait
I think the bat has gone
The night
It always gives me a
Fright.

Rachael Woods (10)
Shevington CP School

Loneliness

When I'm in my bedroom,
I feel the cold of the air.
I hear the rain
Slashing against the window
And when the moon looks down at me,
The rain stops,
The cold has gone
And I fall asleep once more.

Zara Griffiths (9)
Shevington CP School

MEMORIES

Locked up with a key
are my treasures just for me.
They're up above my mouth and nose,
above where I smell a rose.
They're in my mind and I think of them,
they're longer than a sunflower stem.
The first time I made a friend,
my first experience of having to lend.

A toy or a teddy bear,
these are the things I had to share.
My very first day at school,
the time I saw the class fool.
Up into year six
and I learned a lot of new tricks.
These are some of my treasures to behold,
but not all of them have been told.

Charlotte Hurst (10)
Shevington CP School

THE HIDDEN SECRETS OF FRIENDSHIP

I love to play every day,
With my coolest friends.
We hang out near the school,
We are all really cool.
At the shop we buy lots of sweets,
We eat them for a treat.
At the school we climb our tree,
Everything, we can see.
I always have fun with my friends,
Our friendship will never end.

Melissa Boyers (10)
Shevington CP School

Treasures Of Friendship!

Hidden treasures of friendship,
You've got to go deep down to find them,
Travel through their mind,
It might take months, it might even take years,
But eventually surely it will be worth it.

No more fall-outs,
For you or me,
We've covered up the cracks in our friendship,
Now we can get on with sharing our deepest thoughts,
That no one else has ever to be told.

I've found my treasures of friendship,
Now I'll lock them up in a little wooden box
And hide them away forever, in a place somewhere that is secret.

Emma Louise Roberts (10)
Shevington CP School

In My Head At Night

In my head at night,
I go on an RAF flight,
To bomb the Japs
For kicking our butt,
(That's what I think of at night.)

So they are now dead –
In my head.
Every boy's treasured thoughts would be to
Breathe on the moon –
And not end up in doom.
My greatest treasured dreams,
Would be to grow up to be in the Marines.

Jonathan Heaton (11)
Shevington CP School

My Mystical Box

I would put in my box
The roaring sea
The sparkling, shining sun
A slithering, slimy snake
A blue feather off my budgie

I would put in my box
A piece of the moon on a cold winter's night
The taste of a freshly made pizza
The feel of a lamb's wool
The friendship between me and my friend

My box is made out of wood and has gold in the corners
It has a stegosaurus on the lid
Old, rusty, brass hinges
I would sail in my box in a boat
Then jump out and swim in it
Then see the amazing things.

Mark Brennan (9)
Shevington CP School

My Friend

My friend is cool,
We rule the school.
My friend is funny,
Her face is sunny.
We play all day,
In the bushy hay.
Her favourite colour is blue
And I like it too.
She'll be my friend
To the very end.

Katie Sloan (11)
Shevington CP School

SPACE

Once I jumped
To the shiny, sparkly,
Glittery, orange,
Yellow
Sun.

I jumped from the sun
To the yellow,
Sparkly,
Glittery
Moon.

I jumped
From the moon
To the gleaming, glimmering stars,
From Jupiter to Mars,
From Mars back home.

Emma Bibby (10)
Shevington CP School

THE DEAD MOON

As I was going to the moon
Bright stars shone all around
When I landed
It looked gloomy
Large craters were everywhere
I saw footsteps
Around and around
Spotlights shining
Scary sounds
Are there aliens?

Katie Aspey (9)
Shevington CP School

TREASURED MOMENTS

My treasured moments
Are special to me,
Read this poem
And you will see.

When my sister
Was born one night,
I was overjoyed,
I was happy and bright.

I went on holiday to Disneyland,
I went on all the rides.
I won't ever forget that,
It will remain inside.

My first word is special to me,
So is my first laugh.
My first outing I will never forget,
I'll remember my first bath.

All these things will remain in my mind,
Forever and ever they will be inside.

Rachael Hale (10)
Shevington CP School

FRIENDSHIPS

Friendships are very special to me,
Looking at me and Emma Hall you can see,
Some are good, some are bad,
I have a best friend like everyone!

They bring you good luck along your way,
So help each other every day,
Sometimes you fall out, but that's no fun,
Then your heart sinks and weighs a ton!

But in the end you always make up
And it's good when you have your friend back,
This is what happens in a true friendship,
Keep all your friends, they're really fab!

Abigail Telford (10)
Shevington CP School

TREES

Trees, big and old
Their roots stretch for a thousand miles
Their trunks wrinkled like an old woman's face
The wind rushing through their branches
As they sway
Slowly
Slowly
Slowly
Leaves give the tree colour
Like giving an old lady life
Orange
Yellow
Green
Are the colours of the tree
In winter the trees are
Lonely
Lonely
Lonely
For all the animals are asleep
We should care for the trees
Because they
Care for us.

Rachel Crone (10)
Shevington CP School

The Magic Box

In my box
I'll put a motorbike moving into the distance,
Pizza sizzling on my tongue,
A snake sliding through the tall grass.
In my box
I'll put a roar from the crowd when a goal is scored,
My first goal of the season,
A man shooting a building from the distance,
A rabbit bouncing about in grass.
In my box
I'll put some hot soup dripping down my mouth,
Some flames dancing in the fire,
A dolphin diving into the deep dark sea.

James Taylor (9)
Shevington CP School

Journey Through Life

There he sits
In front of the fire,
Thinking of his journey through life.
Like a tree so still and tall.
Fun he had,
Mischievous nights,
Holidays with laughter.
The bits he could have done better.
Cold winter nights in front of the fire,
Shining stars up above,
Late nights outside.
Like a cold standing statue,
The journey through life!

Natalie Johnson (9)
Shevington CP School

The Journey Through The Year

Summer days when the sky is blue,
The days are hot, sweaty too.

Autumn days when the grass is jewelled,
The leaves are falling off the trees,
Playing with the conkers all day long.

Winter days when the trees are bare,
The days are cold,
Mountains are at the freezing point.

Spring days when the flowers are out,
Fairies and elves too,
Playing skipping on the field.

Lucy Crawshaw (10)
Shevington CP School

My Special Box

In my special box, I will put a golden fish
and my best food on a silver dish.

A gold crown
and my first frown.

A gleaming blue pool,
that's warm and cool.

A magical land,
the soft, silky sand.

The beating of a heart,
a delicious jam tart.

Chad Wilson (10)
Shevington CP School

My Whisperful Box

I would whisper into my box,
A tickling touch that made trouble,
A wicked witch wanting wonderful things to wander
And a slide of a seal on a sandy beach.
I would whisper into my box,
A tattoo on a tall, terrible man,
The smell of sausages sizzling in a pan
And a crash in the kitchen while cooking custard.
My box is made of magic spells and potions,
The lid is made of half the moon and half the sun,
It shines in the day and glows in the night.
If I went in my box,
I would walk with dinosaurs,
Make a magic spell with a batty witch,
Eat with fairies
And go to a goblin disco and dance all night long!

Rachel Holgate (10)
Shevington CP School

The Dump

Twisted metal
And bits of kettle
Twisted pipes that look like a creeping spider
Purple steel
Banana peel
Pipes tangled in the paper and cardboard
It's like walking into a bin!

Steven Grimshaw (10)
Shevington CP School

Treasured Moments

My hidden treasure is under the sea,
Waiting, ready just for me.
All locked up in my heart,
Me and my thoughts will never be apart.

My first birthday with a friend,
I hope these thoughts will never end.
My first holiday in Cyprus,
All my fights with my diapers.

My first taste of chocolate pudding,
When I dressed up, I looked stunning.
My first ever day at school,
I thought was really cool!
Straight away I played with the sandpit,
I didn't like the bikes a bit.

Robyn Jennifer Bragg (10)
Shevington CP School

Treasure

Treasure is shining and gleaming,
Treasure is gold and silver,
Treasure is diamonds and crystals,
Treasure is pearls and rubies,
Treasure is coins, necklaces and bracelets,
Treasure is a ring,
Treasure is a gold crown,
Treasure is the love of everyone.

Thomas Sutherland (10)
Shevington CP School

MY SPECIAL BOX

In my special box I will put
The sounds of my long lost great grandad
The planets in space which no one has seen
Everyone in the world who is nice

In my special box I will put
My favourite day at the beach
The magical clouds in the sky
All the days in my life

In my special box I will put
The smell of my great grandma's perfume
The touch of the sun when it's not hot
And a bit of the Earth.

Michelle Staunton (9)
Shevington CP School

A TREASURE FROM FRANCE

My souvenir from my holiday in France
Is told to give me lots of chance,
It has four leaves, it's meant to have three,
A tiny little plant that is hard to see.
I never stopped hunting for hours on end,
But after a while it got found by my friend,
My favourite thing, have you guessed?
It's my four-leaf clover because it is better than the rest.

Megan Ruth Whittaker (10)
Shevington CP School